GreatCentsBooks

For permission requests, please contact:
GreatCents Books
bteich@greatcents.org

Edited by: Blake Teichmeier

Junior Editor: Augustine Hanson

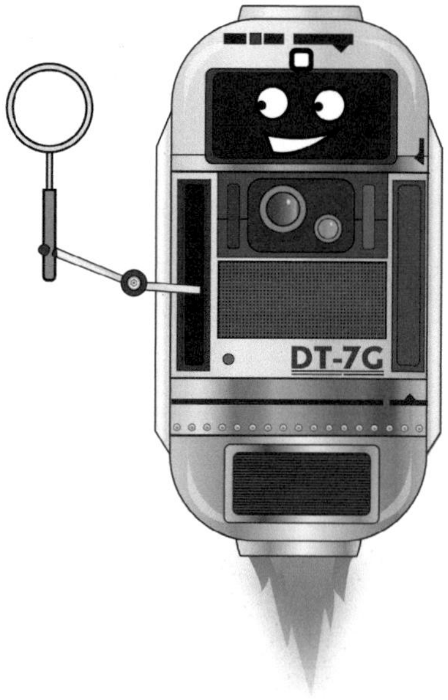

Printed in the United States of America.

ISBN: 978-1-971213-06-4

First Edition: January 12th, 2025

To Scott Johnson, who took me in and mentored me when I needed it most, I wouldn't be here without you.

This book is part of the series called **Galactic Growth**. Our goal is to help you think about your **mind & money.**

Who are you dedicating your work on this book to:

Table of Contents

This book belongs to:

Galactic Growth!

SEL and Personal Finance

How to Handle Stress and Risk!

Written and Illustrated by:
Blake Teichmeier

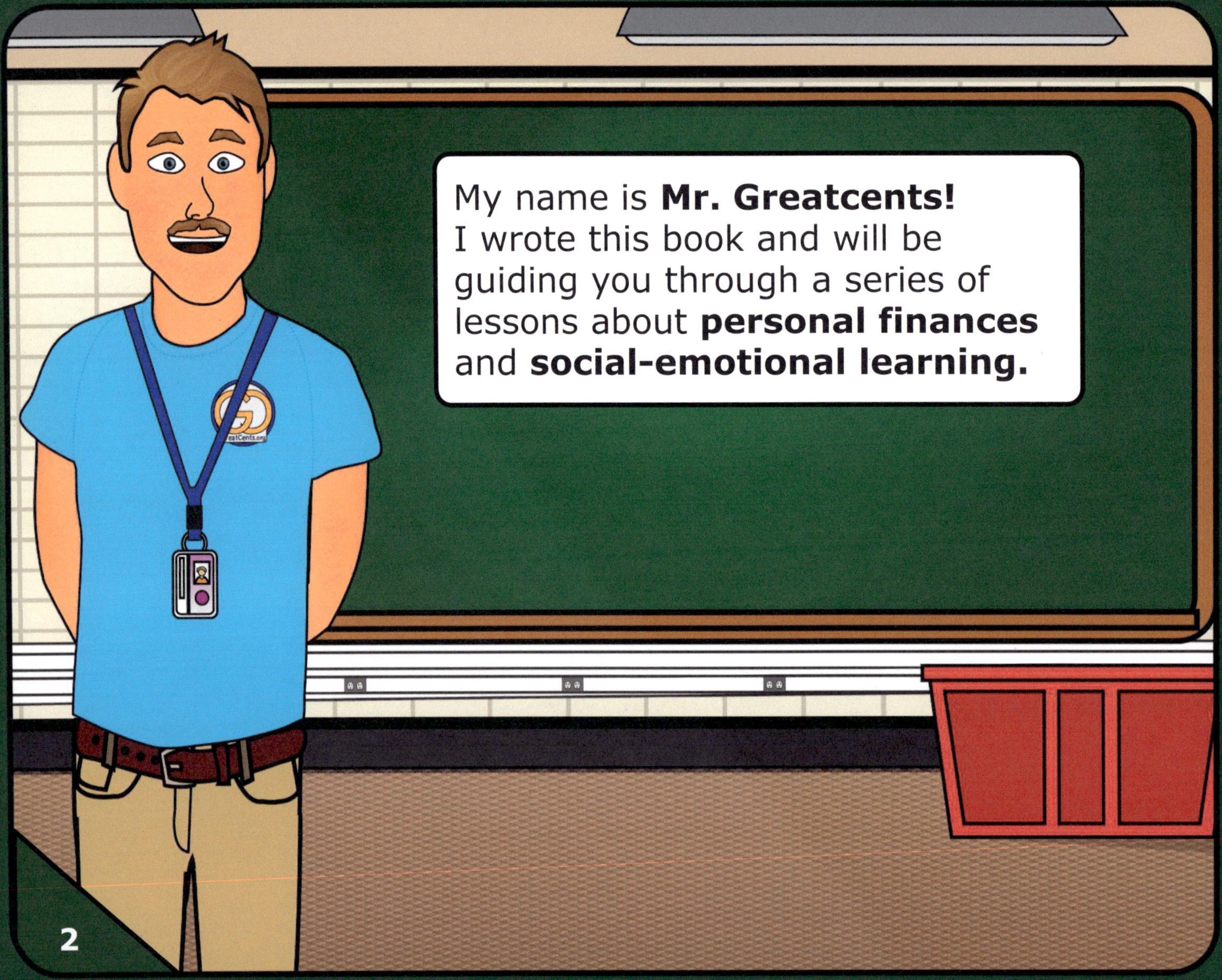
My name is **Mr. Greatcents!** I wrote this book and will be guiding you through a series of lessons about **personal finances** and **social-emotional learning.**

You are getting older, and with that comes **new responsibilities**. You will need to be more aware of your **mind**, the choices you make, and your **money**, and the way you spend and save your money. Join me as we leave our familiar world behind and venture into a universe of learning!

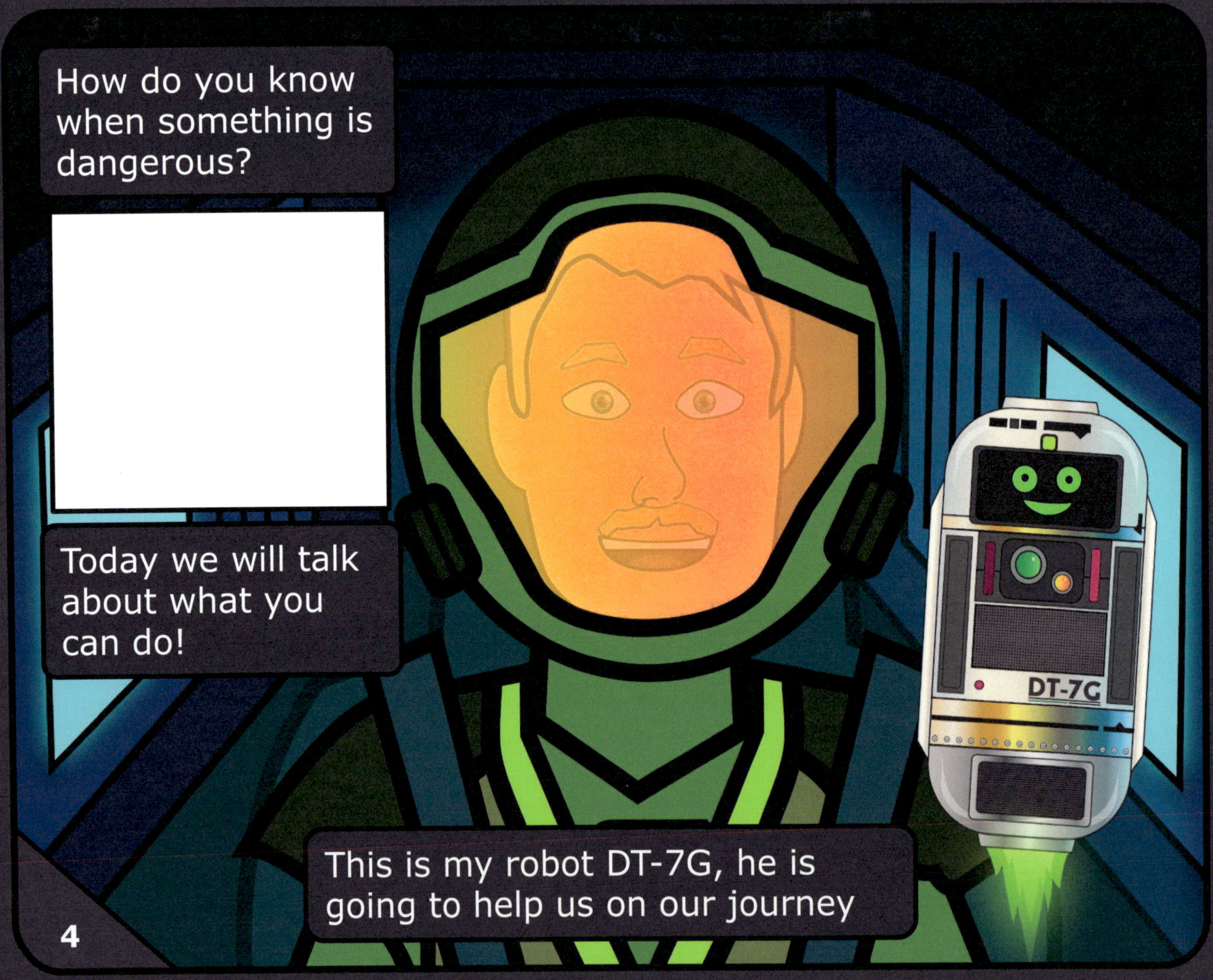
How do you know when something is dangerous?
Today we will talk about what you can do!
This is my robot DT-7G, he is going to help us on our journey
DT-7G

Galactic Growth!

Social Emotional Learning & Personal Finances

How to Handle Stress and Risk!

Our Goal:
Learn strategies for handling **risk** and **stress** in our lives.

Step 1:
Recognize how stress can cause us to react.

Step 2:
Understand thoughts, feelings and behaviors are how they are connected.

Step 3:
Identify the ways a person can handle risk personally & financially.

Step 4:
Investigate insurance and fill out policies for stress and risk.

1 2 3

Books are awesome because they are able to take us places! **Reading is a power** that allows you to learn from so many brilliant people throughout all of time. It also opens you to stories that fill us with wonder and imagination!

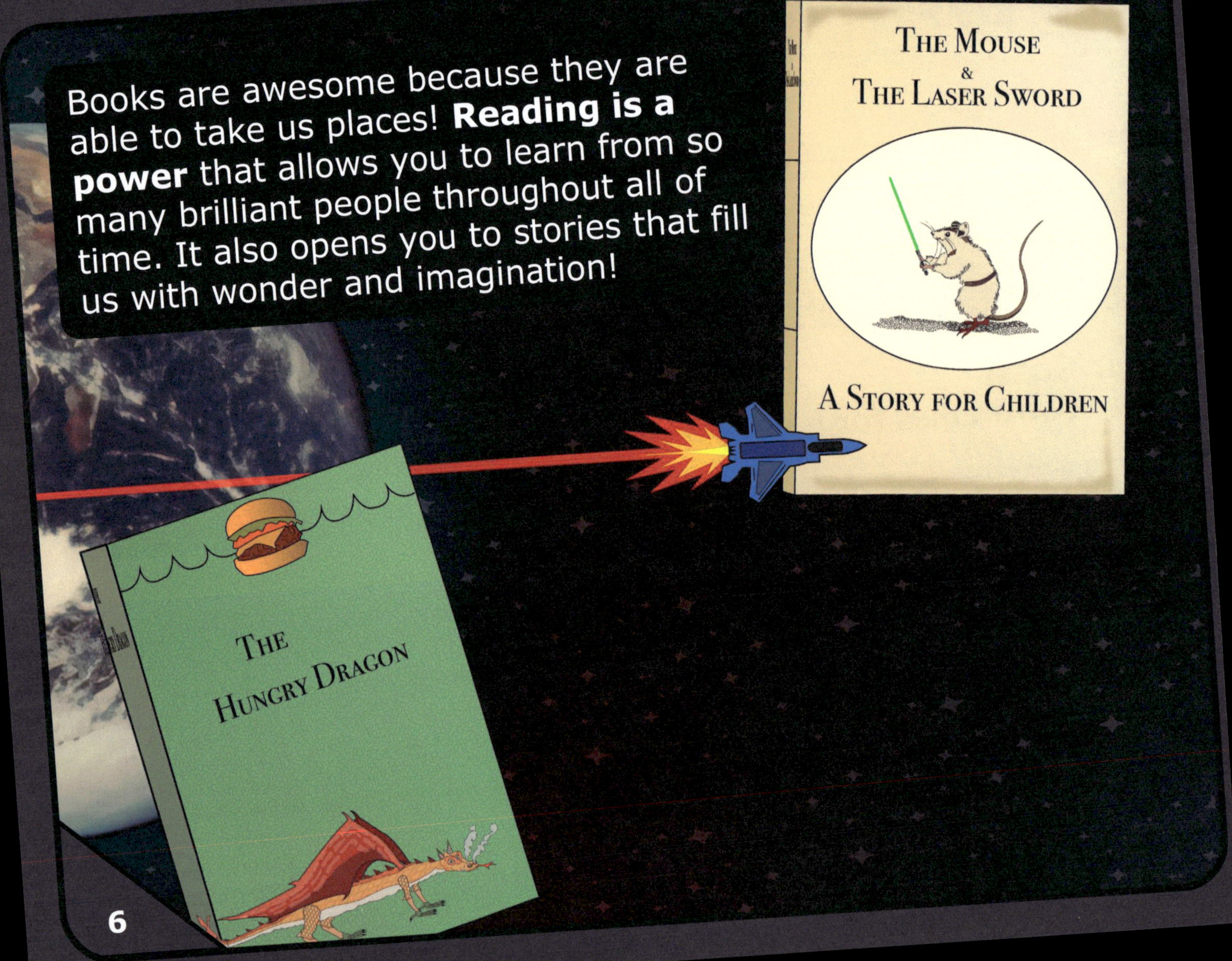

"It seemed to me that a careful examination of the room and the lawn might possibly reveal some traces of this mysterious individual. You know my methods, Watson."
Oh! You caught me listening to my audiobook, it's a Sherlock Holmes story. **When you're traveling, how do you pass the time?**
7

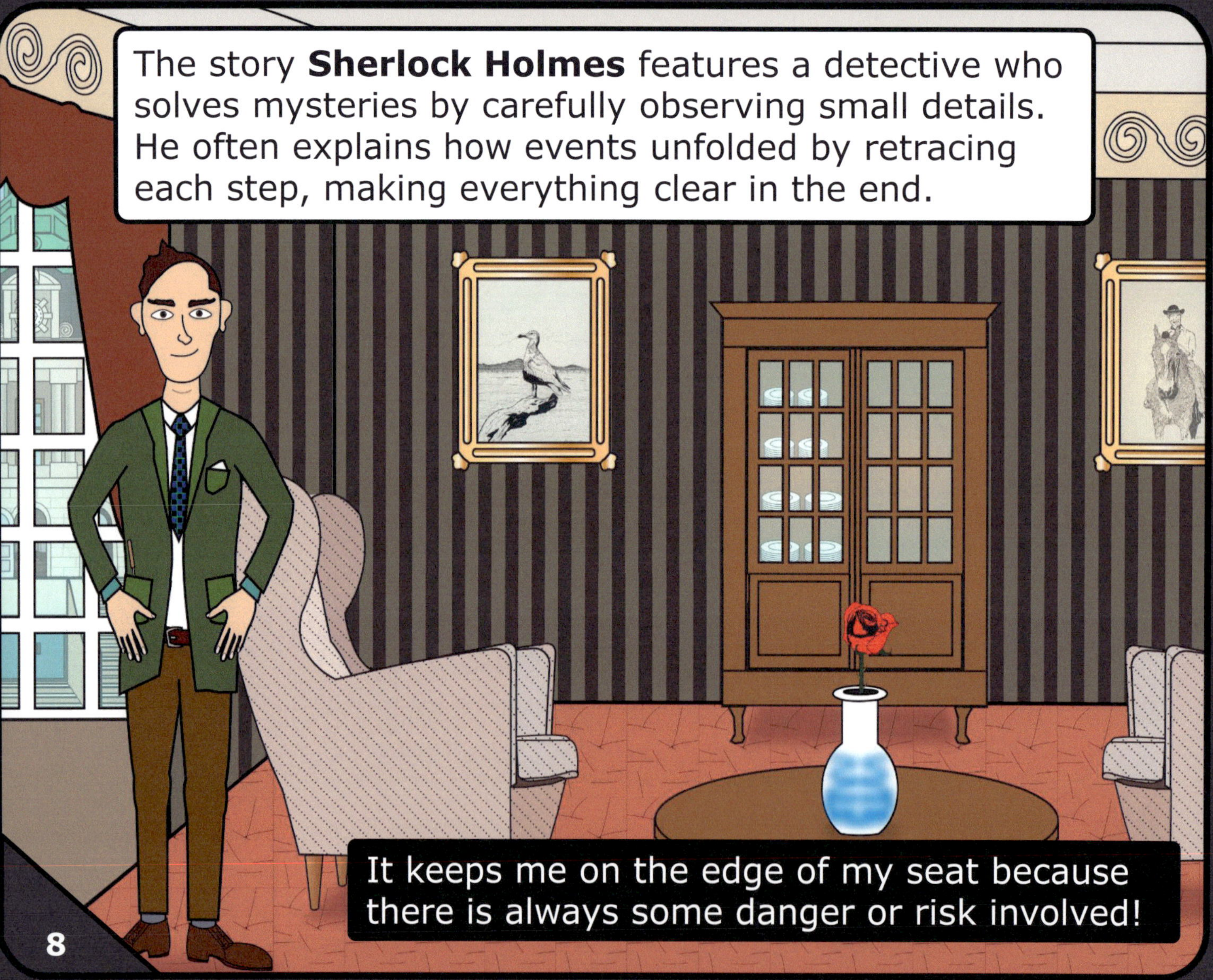
The story **Sherlock Holmes** features a detective who solves mysteries by carefully observing small details. He often explains how events unfolded by retracing each step, making everything clear in the end.
It keeps me on the edge of my seat because there is always some danger or risk involved!

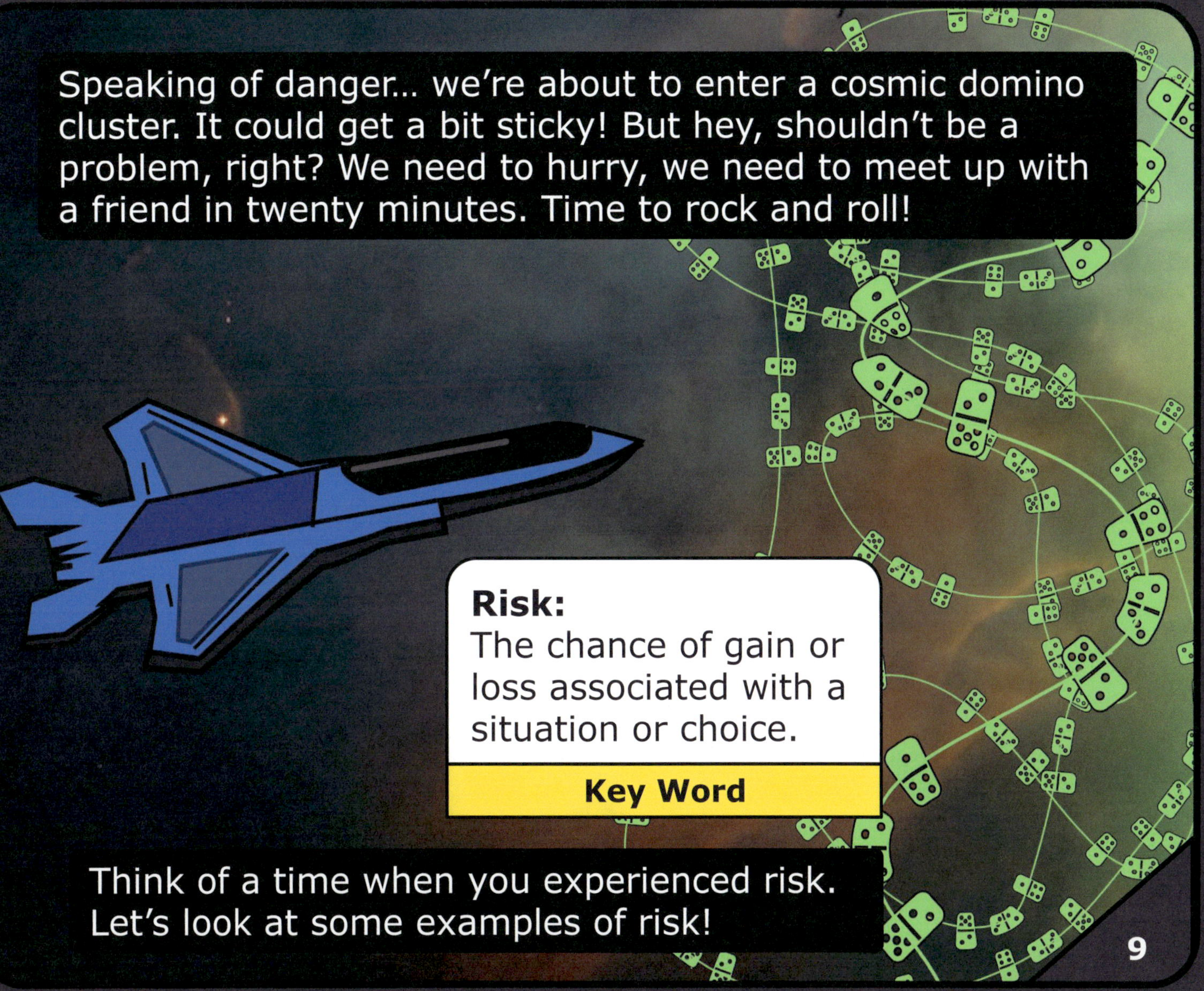

Speaking of danger... we're about to enter a cosmic domino cluster. It could get a bit sticky! But hey, shouldn't be a problem, right? We need to hurry, we need to meet up with a friend in twenty minutes. Time to rock and roll!
Risk:
The chance of gain or loss associated with a situation or choice.
Key Word
Think of a time when you experienced risk. Let's look at some examples of risk!

Health Risks

We all have bodies and we all get sick or hurt at times. This is why it is so important to take care of ourselves. The risk of getting hurt is not only painful, but also expensive.

What are some things a person would go to the hospital for?

Property Risks

We all have stuff and over time it can wear down or get damaged. This is why it is so important to take care of our things. It can cost a lot to replace our property when it breaks.

What is something valuable you own? How do you care for it?

Auto Risks

We all need to get from one place to another. Cars are powerful machines, yet they also can cause a lot of damage when things go wrong. This is why it is so important to follow the road signs and drive safely!
What are some dangers that come with vehicles?

Life Risks

We all live with others, people we love. Sadly Some of us have experienced the loss of a loved one. This can completely change a person's life. This is why it is so important to appreciate your loved ones, have a plan and get help when life is difficult. **Who are the people that take care of you?**

Risk is a real thing that affects people every day. This storm is getting more intense...
Beep...

Blast it! WE ARE STUCK!
This is just rotten... we never should have taken this path!
So dumb! ... Now I need to send out a distress call..
This is going to make us late...
DT-7C

Oh... Wow, the distress robot is here already... We should be on our way in just a few minutes... I didn't expect that...
Hey crew, I want to apologize for the way I reacted.
I feel pretty embarrassed now. I said some things when I was angry and that is not how I usually am.
DT-7C

I made a mistake. I can't change the past, but I can reflect on what happened. I want to have a better reaction next time. This will help me in the future.
Self-Management:
The ability to manage your own emotions, thoughts, and behaviors to achieve goals.
Key Word
DT-7G
Let's look at how this happened!

Risk and **danger** can create pressure, which in turn causes **stress**.

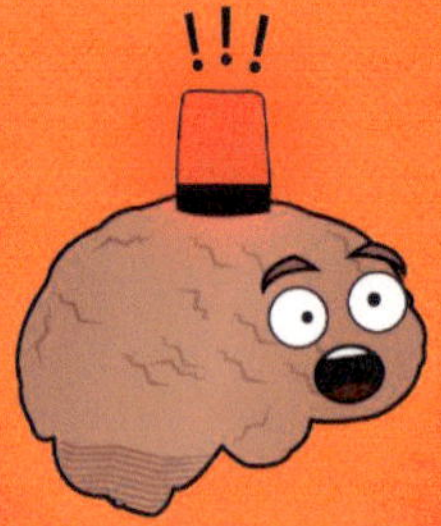

Stress:
The body's response to physical, mental, or emotional pressure.

Key Word

Our brains do their best to help us as we live life. Most of the time, this is great because it helps us with everyday tasks. For example, when walking you don't have to tell your legs what to do. **However, this can sometimes backfire with stress. It can cause our minds to go into automatic mode!**

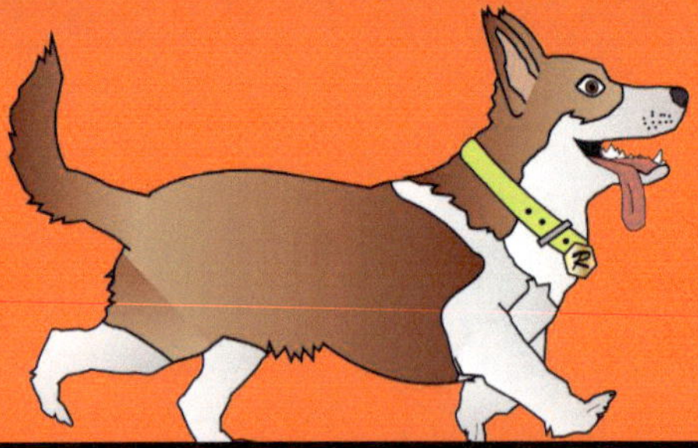

Share a definition of what risk and stress are in your own words!

Risk:	Stress:

"Name it to tame it." One of the most powerful things you can do to have control over your overwhelming feelings is to **label it!**

Illustrate four situations that could cause a kid to feel stress!

Risk:	Risk:	Risk:	Risk:
How would you feel?	How would you feel?	How would you feel?	How would you feel?

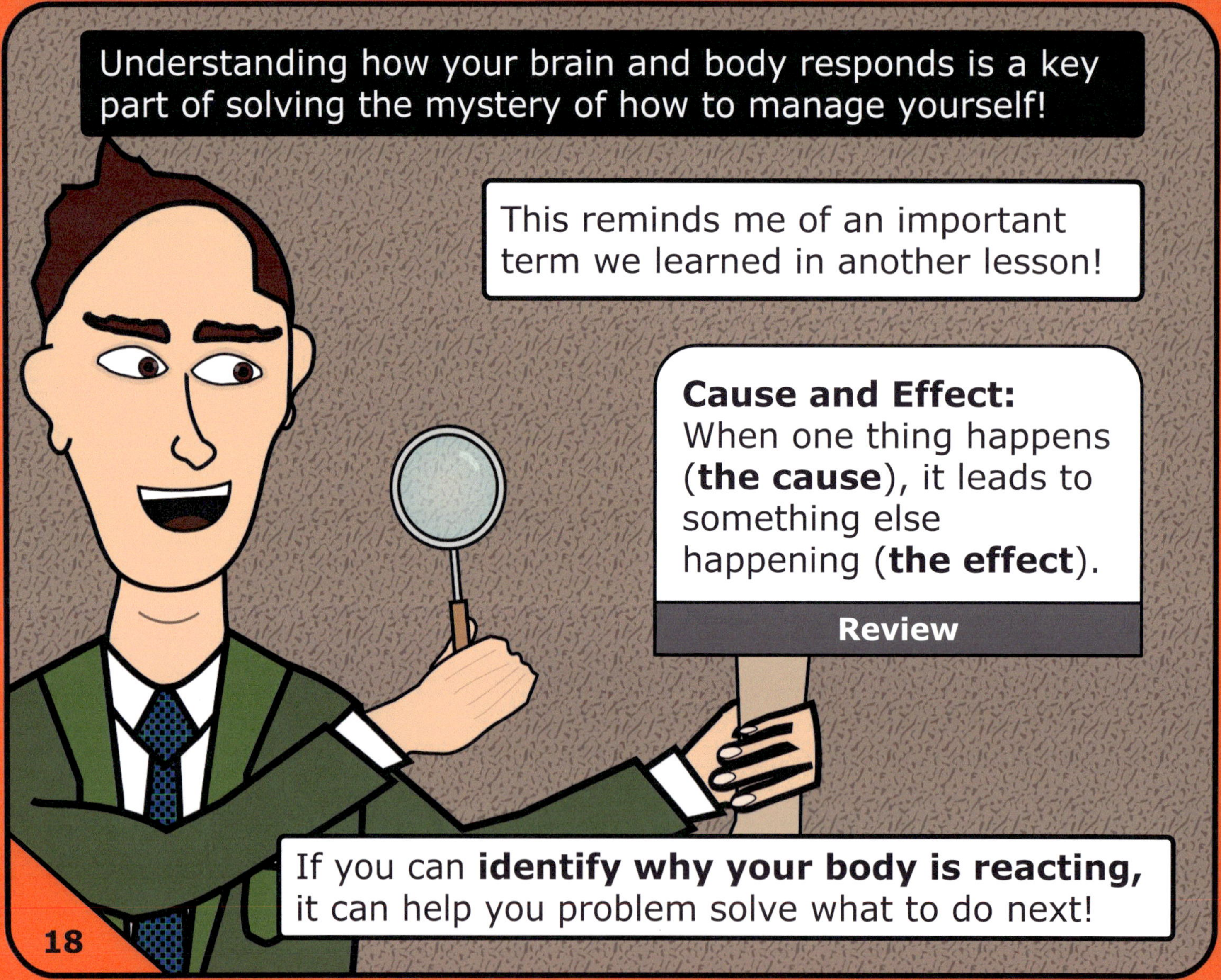
Understanding how your brain and body responds is a key part of solving the mystery of how to manage yourself!
This reminds me of an important term we learned in another lesson!
Cause and Effect: When one thing happens (**the cause**), it leads to something else happening (**the effect**).
Review
If you can **identify why your body is reacting,** it can help you problem solve what to do next!

What is really important is what you do when you feel these emotions. When we understand why we are doing what we are doing, it helps us stay in control!

Quick note! Everyone has emotions, and that is part of being a human being. Sherlock, a master detective, would even have times when he got angry because he wasn't able to solve the case.

Here are some of the ways people can react to stress:

Fight Mode:

Your body senses risk and reacts by getting ready to attack in order to protect itself.

Your Body

Physically:

- Increased heart rate
- Muscles become tense
- Heightened awareness

Mental & Emotion:

- Feelings of anger
- Feeling irritable
- Feeling assertive
- Wanting control

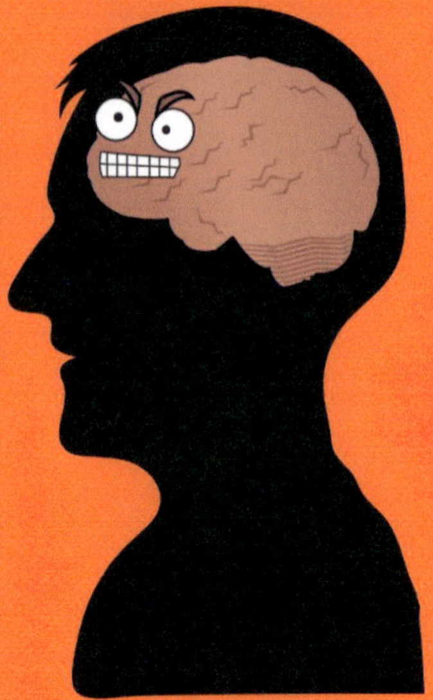

Flight Mode:

Your body senses risk and tries to escape or avoid the threat.

Your Body

Physically:

- Rapid breathing
- Nausea
- Discomfort
- Restlessness

Mental & Emotion:

- Feelings of anxiety
- Feeling fearful
- Feeling overwhelmed
- Wanting to escape

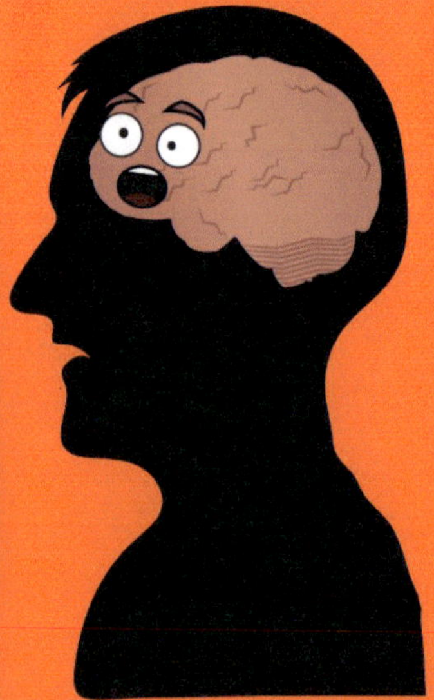

Fight Mode:

Take deep breaths - Box Breathing ☐
Breath in 4 seconds, **Hold** 4 seconds, **Exhale** for 4 seconds, **Hold** 4 seconds.
Repeat for **one** to **ten** minutes.

- This will help relax your brain and make thoughtful choices.

Let's practice this right now!
☐ Set a timer for 5 minutes ☐ Box Breathe
How did it make you feel?

How could this help you?

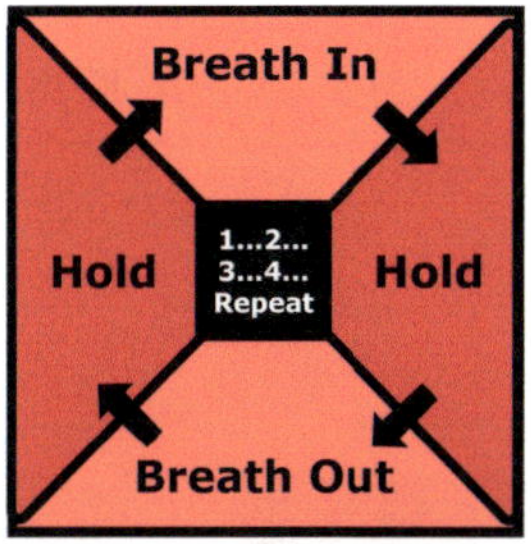

Flight Mode:

If Then Statements "**If** (describe situation), **then** (action)."
Step 1: Identify a situation that causes you to respond with fear.
Step 2: Think of how you would like to respond instead.
Step 3: Make a phrase that reminds you how you want to respond.
Ex. "If I'm scared to talk to a friend, then I'll write it out first."
Make your own "If... Then..." statement!
If

Then

How could this help you?

Freeze Mode:

When your body senses risk, it shuts down or feels stuck.

Your Body

Physically:

- Body feels frozen
- Heart rate slows down
- Trouble moving
- Trouble speaking

Mental & Emotion:

- Feeling shocked
- Feeling numb or blank
- Wanting to avoid

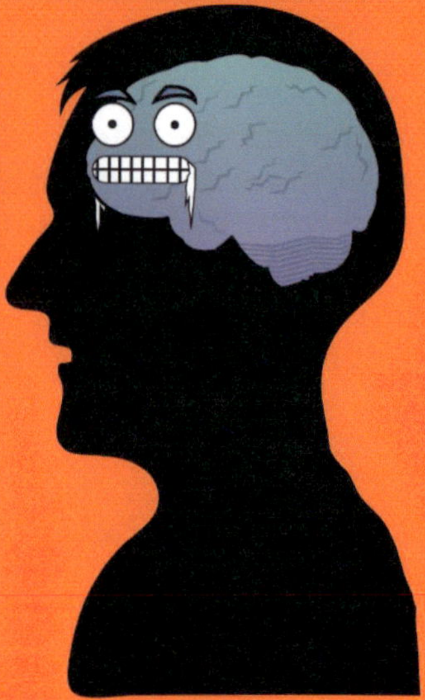

Fawn Mode:

When your body senses risk and tries to please others to avoid conflict or danger.

Your Body

Physically:

- Nervous feelings
- Soft voice or posture
- Tense body

Mental & Emotion:

- Feeling fear of others
- People-pleasing
- Wanting to make others happy, even when you don't want to

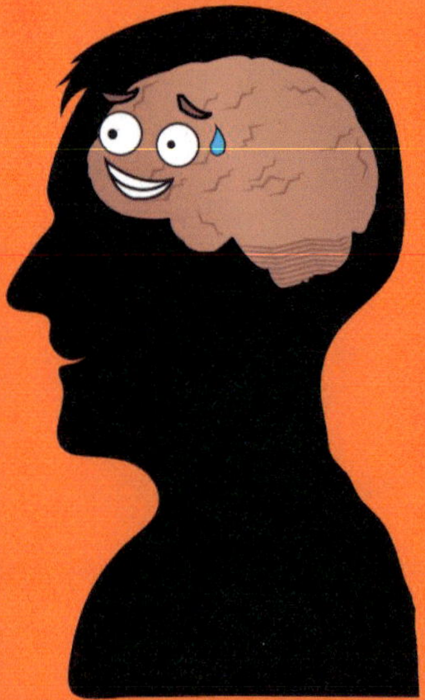

Freeze Mode:

When your body feels like it is stuck you need to:

• Get Grounded! Wiggle your fingers and toes! Wake up your system.

Test your 5 Senses! Test this right now!

Sight – What do you see?

Hearing – What do you hear?

Smell – What do you smell?

Taste – What do you taste?

Touch – What do you feel?

How could this help you?

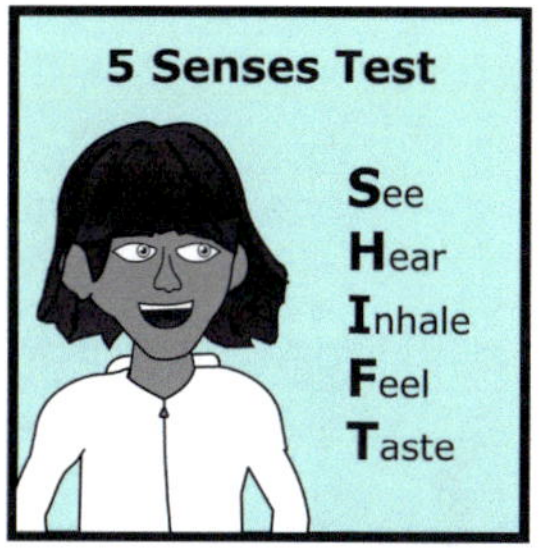

Fawn Mode:

When you feel pressure to make an uncomfortable choice, set boundaries!

• Know your limits and what you want, think of these as **Fences**.

Saying "no" isn't mean, it's healthy.

• Know who you trust and want to help guide you. **Fences have Gates!**

Say "yes" to the right people builds trust!

Who is someone you consider safe to share with?

Why?

Reflection time!

Thought:
There was a high chance we were going to be late. That was stressful.

Feeling:
This put me into fight mode, I was angry.

Behavior:
I shouted and threw a bit of a fit.

If I get into a stressful situation like this, **then** I will stop, take a minute to **box breathe** and think through my options.

Beep-Beep!

Describe a time you were stressed?
What did you do to handle the situation?

Step 1:
Recognize how stress can cause us to react.

How to Handle Stress!

Now that we have looked at **stress** let's take a look at a more detailed way of handling our inner world. It is a way of mapping how our **thoughts** translate to our **feelings** and **behaviors**.

The TFB in Me: The process of recognizing the cycle of **thoughts**, **feelings** and **behaviors** that shape our lives.

Key Word

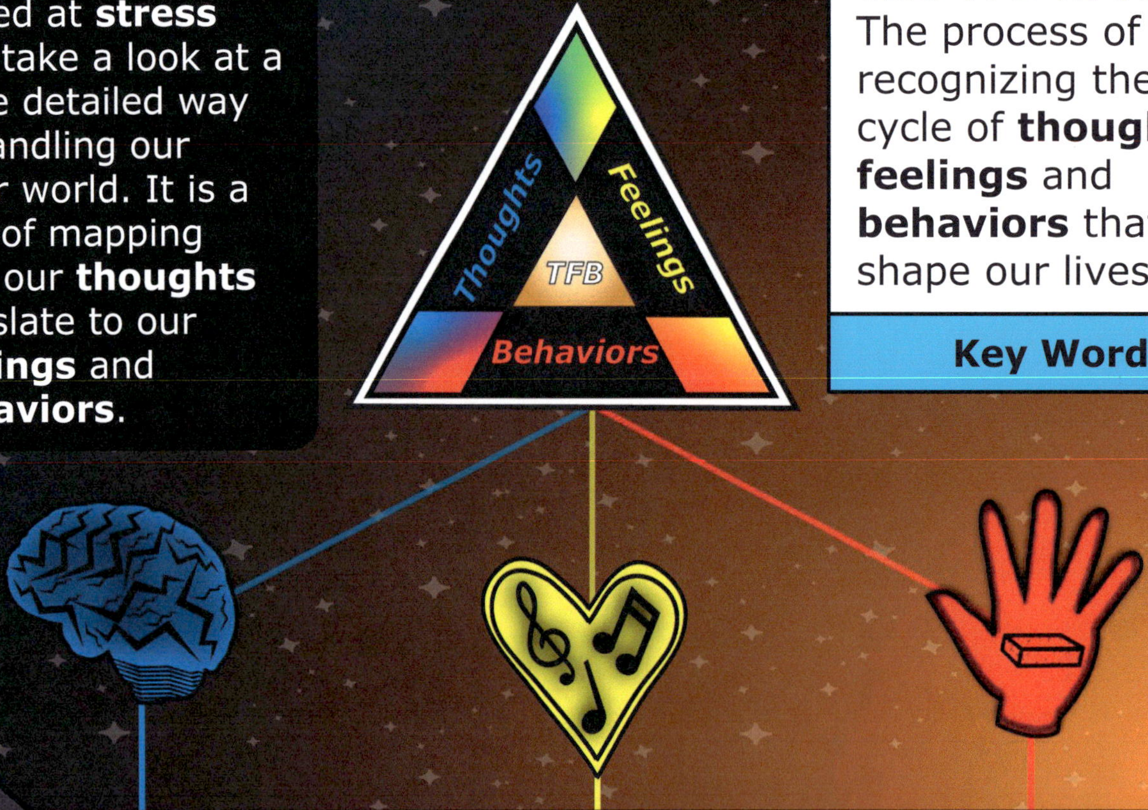

Here is an example!

Situation:
Jessica left work late and is in a hurry to get to a friends party.

Thought:
"I am going to be late to the party... my friend is going to be so mad!"

Feeling:
Nervous
Worried
Anxious

Behavior:
Jessica might go over the speed limit while driving to the party. Risky!

We talked about the way your brain reacts to stress to protect you. Now we are going to talk about the **power** of **thoughts**, **feelings** and how they shape your **behavior**. We need to stop and look at the clues!

To manage our stress the first step is to recognize our **thoughts**!

Your brain is an incredible gift! It has the ability to process choices, store memories, and keep you alive.

Thoughts:

Ideas that are being processed in your mind to make sense of the world.

The ability to understand through concepts, decisions, problem solving, memories and beliefs.

Key Word

Your thoughts are like electricity traveling over paths called neural pathways. The more you do or think, the stronger the pathway; you shape in your mind!

That's why it's important to be thoughtful about your thoughts! What you hold in your mind shapes how you learn, feel, and grow.

Wait... did I study for this quiz?

That's Mike!

Hungry!

Something smells... is that me?

The answer is...dolphins!

(Music on repeat)

Did I lock the door when I left the house this morning?

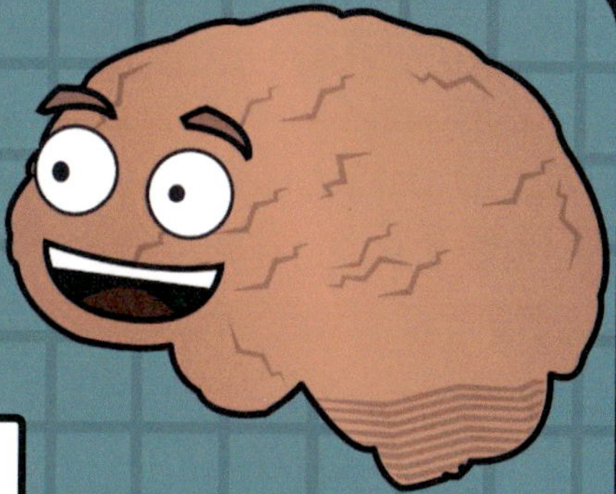

A mind of its own!
All day long our brains are talking to us. That is normal. They are trying to help us make sense of the world and ourselves. This is **Self Talk**!

Self Talk:
The thoughts and words you tell yourself every day. These shape your beliefs, confidence, and behavior.

Key Word

What are some thoughts you have had today? Try to share 4 things!

Notice how people are drawn to sad, scary or serious news? When it comes to our thoughts it is actually one of the ways our brain tries to help protect us!

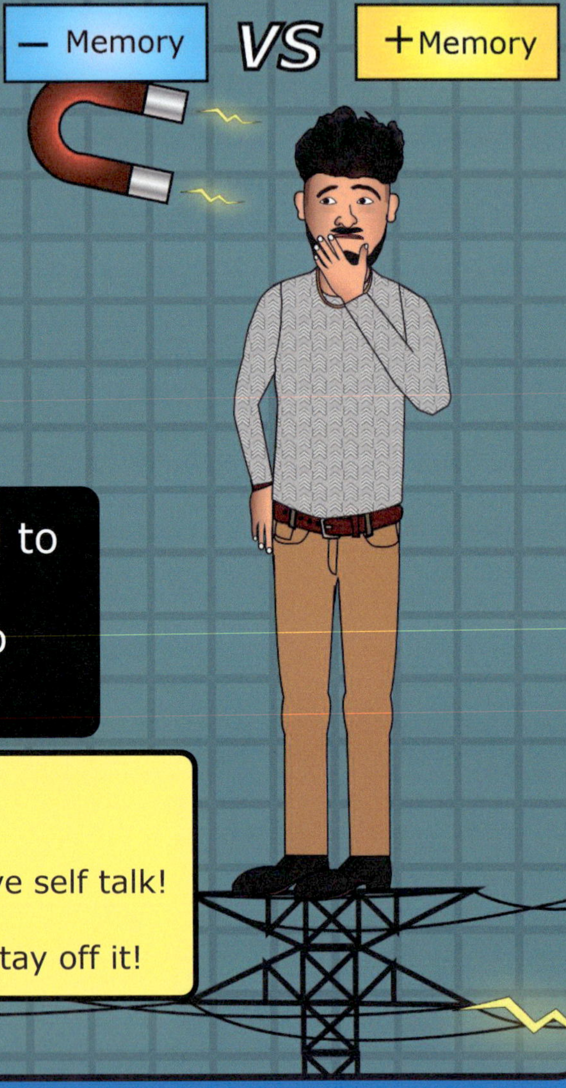

Negativity Bias:
The mind naturally focuses more attention on negative experiences or information.

Key Word

In order to manage stress, we need to maintain a balance of positive and negative thoughts in our minds. Too much negativity can make us sick!

Here are some tips!

- Practice **gratitude** (thankfulness).
- **Challenge** negative thoughts with positive self talk!
- Take time each day to **rest** your mind.
- **Be mindful** of your social media use or stay off it!

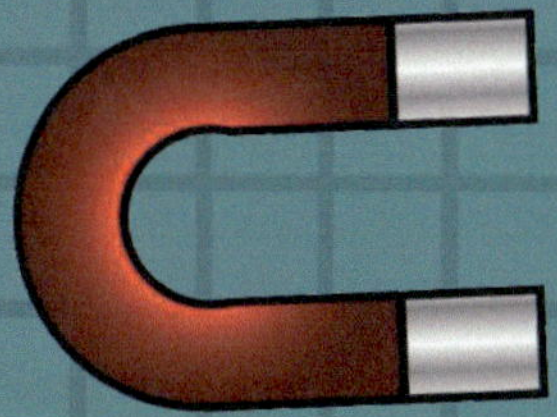

How can you protect yourself from negativity bias?

What are some positive things you could think about with self talk?

Quick tips for your thoughts:

Your brain needs:

Oxygen - Get outside and breathe in from fresh air.
Nutrition - Eating healthy foods to fuel your mind.
Sleep - Rest helps your brain recharge and process your day.
Exercise - Being active helps your blood flow to your brain.

To manage our stress the second step is to read our **feelings**!

Feelings:
Sensations experienced in your body as a response to your thoughts.
The most common feelings are happiness, fear, sadness, anger, disgust, and surprise.

Key Word

Your heart is a muscle in your chest, but when people talk about it, they are often referring to your ability to feel emotions.

Thoughts charge our feelings like music. This causes our emotions to move and flow, with many different notes, just like a song.

There are no bad feelings.
Each one is an indicator of what is happening in our minds.
If feelings become overwhelming, we can turn down the music with our thoughts and actions.

Having more descriptive words can help us express our emotions!

Happy
(1) Calm
(2) Content
(3) Excited
(4) Cheerful
(5) Glad
(6) Proud
(7) Thankful
(8) Joyful
(9) Energetic
(10) Ecstatic

Scared
(1) Nervous
(2) Worried
(3) Unsure
(4) Afraid
(5) Shaky
(6) Anxious
(7) Startled
(8) Overwhelmed
(9) Terrified
(10) Panicked

Sad
(1) Down
(2) Disappointed
(3) Lonely
(4) Hurt
(5) Upset
(6) Blue
(7) Discouraged
(8) Tearful
(9) Miserable
(10) Heartbroken

Mad
(1) Annoyed
(2) Frustrated
(3) Irritated
(4) Angry
(5) Mad
(6) Upset
(7) Fed up
(8) Furious
(9) Seething
(10) Livid

Disgusted
(1) Uncomfortable
(2) Grossed out
(3) Bothered
(4) Offended
(5) Sickened
(6) Disturbed
(7) Repulsed
(8) Creeped out
(9) Nauseous
(10) Appalled

Surprised
(1) Curious
(2) Shocked
(3) Confused
(4) Amazed
(5) Startled
(6) Impressed
(7) Caught off guard
(8) Stunned
(9) Unexpected
(10) Speechless

How are you feeling today?
Our thoughts shape our feelings, but so does our physical health!

When we are worn down our emotions can take on a life of their own. Beware when you are:

Hungry
Angry
Lonely
Tired

Sometimes the best thing you can do to handle stress is having a snack or taking a nap.

How are you feeling today? Why?
(use the chart to be specific)

"Feelings are temporary"
What does this mean?

Identify what this person is feeling:

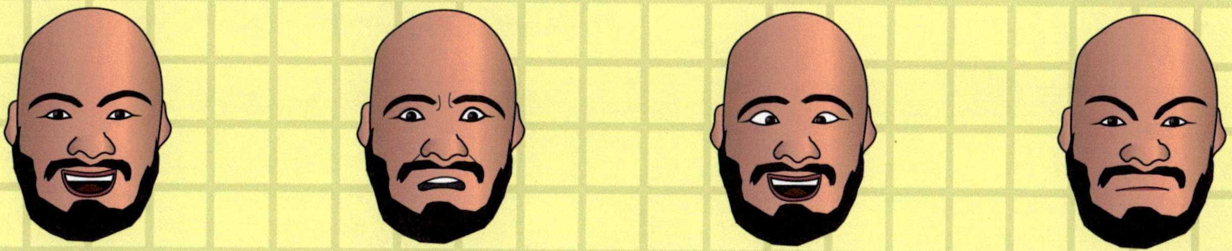

To manage our stress, the next step is to control our **behaviors**!

Behaviors:
Actions taken either on purpose or as a reaction to our thoughts and feelings.

Key Word

This is where your inner world becomes visible to others. Your thoughts and feelings are inside you, but your behaviors are what people can see.

Your behaviors are like bricks. You use them to build habits and shape how others see you. They are concrete, and they can have a lasting impact on others, for good or for bad.

Behaviors are the actions people see. They show how we respond to our thoughts and feelings. When we slow down and make thoughtful choices, we can use our behaviors to build trust, solve problems, and handle stress in a healthy way.

"Why!" To "Why?"

Sometimes it can be easy to get frustrated with the behavior of ourselves and others. "Why did I do that!?" **However, one thing we can do to help ourselves is to get curious instead of angry.**

Why did that hurt my feelings when Jennifer said...

Why do I worry so much about what people think of me?

What is a "Why!" You could change to a "Why?" How would you think about it differently?

We naturally build habits! In general, if you do something consistently for a month it will likely become a habit!

Habit:
A habit is something you do regularly, often without thinking, as part of your daily activities.

Key Word

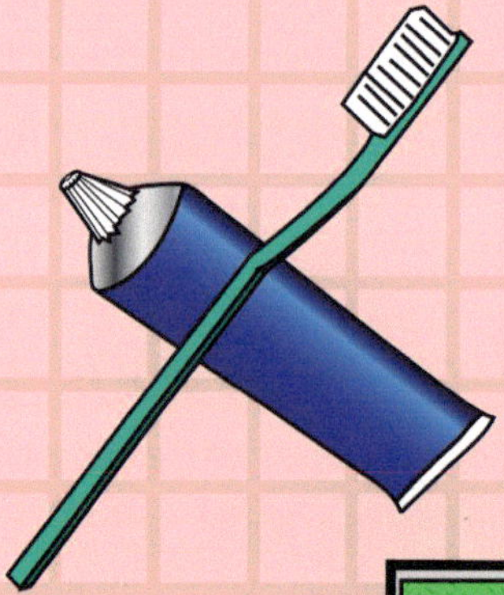

Everyday you are shaping your future self!
Here are some great habits to build:

- Learning interesting things
- Stay organized
- Eat healthy food
- Find fun exercise
- Follow a bedtime

Quick tips for building habits: GROW

Goal: Write down your new habit and post it somewhere!

Routine: Find a time to do this activity everyday.

Observe: Mark each time you complete it, get a streak!

Win: When you reach your goal, treat yourself to an award!

Now make a GROW Goals for each of these areas!

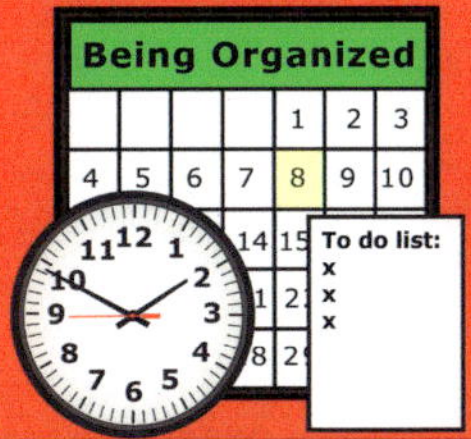	**Goal:**	**Routine:**	**Observe:**	**Win:**
	**Goal:**	**Routine:**	**Observe:**	**Win:**
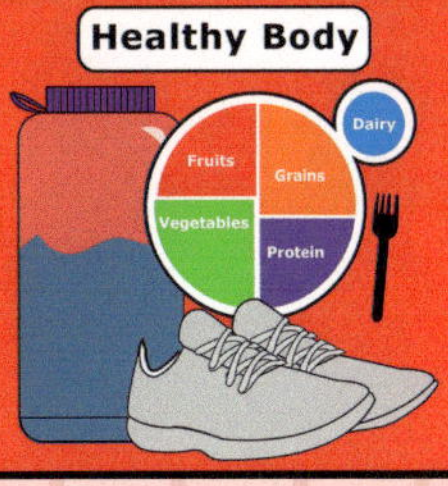	**Goal:**	**Routine:**	**Observe:**	**Win:**

Self-Management requires us to examine ourselves and choose how we will act! Small changes in your **TFB** can change your life! Here are some examples!

Thought:

- "I should listen to others."
- "This is hard, but I can try my best."
- "Getting angry won't help this situation."
- "I can learn from this."

Feeling:

- Paying attention to how you feel inside.
- Pausing before reacting
- Naming your feeling
- Choosing a calm or positive attitude

Behavior:

- Try again.
- Ask for help.
- Help someone else.
- Take a deep breath.

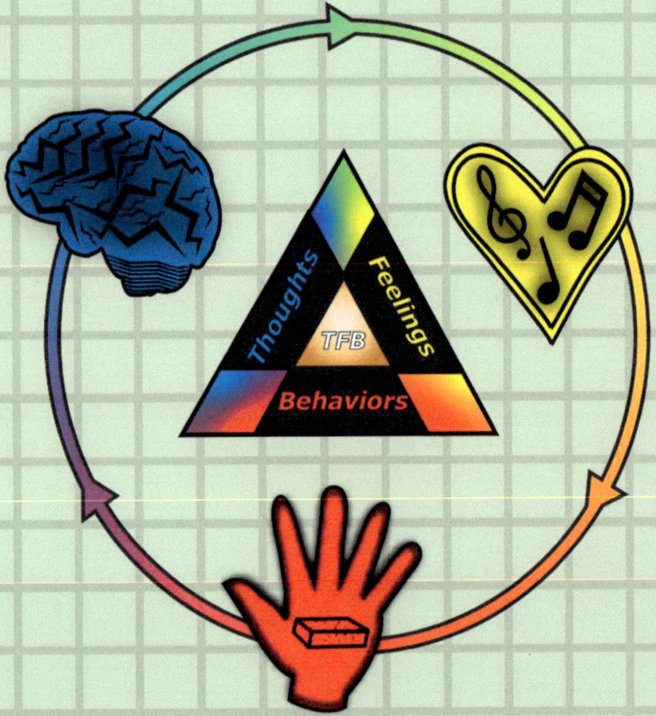

Now that you are aware of your TFB you are like a detective! Your brains is always trying to figure out how to deal with different life **situations**. This is where you can break down the facts!

Situation:
What is happening?
Who is involved?

Thoughts:
What is the risk?
How should I handle the risk?

Feeling:
How will this likely make me feel?
What type of attitude do I have right now?

Behavior:
What should I do?
When?

Test it right now! Think of a situation!

"What if suddenly I need to make a quick choice? What should I do?"

Life happens fast! So when it comes to **self-management** one of the best things you can do is to **slow down.** You owe it to yourself to **take the time** to make a decision that you are confident in. We have a phrase to help us!

STOP. SCAN. PLAN

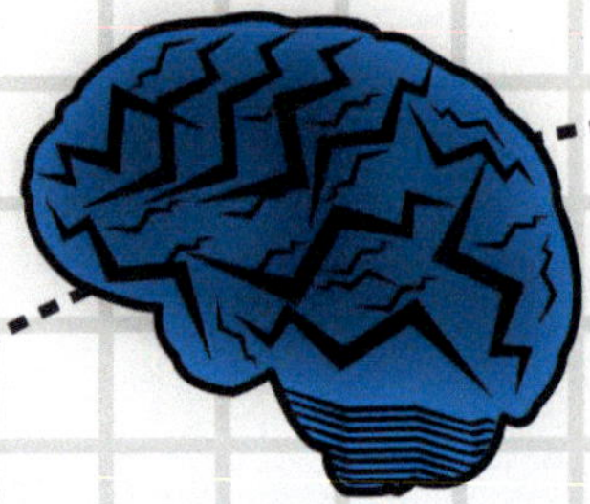

Stop. Breathe....
Take a moment to help your mind **relax**.

Recognize the Situation
Try to understand what is happening.

Think about the opportunity and risk
What could you get, what could you lose?

Take a moment to sense your feelings
Why are you feeling this way? How are others feeling?

What are my options
What do I have control over and what do I need to rely on others for?

Make your plan.
After thinking through your TFB, make your choice!

Let's practice this by observing Leona.

Situation: Leona is really angry with her brother Pawnee. He has been embarrassing her infront of her friends. She really wants to get back at him.

Her Thoughts

Pawnee is trying to embarrass me infront of my friends. He is being a real jerk. **I need to do something about it.**

Her Feelings

Angry, embarrassed, frustrated, hurt.

The Moment of Choice!

Fight Mode

My turn now, I'll embarrass him!

Mean

Leona starts spreading rumors!

Kids are making jokes about Pawnee.

OR

STOP. SCAN. PLAN

Stop! Box Breath
☐ 1...2...3...4...

Pawnee embarrassed me.
Why did he do it?
What can I control?
Let's make a plan!

Hopeful, Interested

Leona asks to talk with Pawnee privately.

Let's see how these two ways of handling it went.

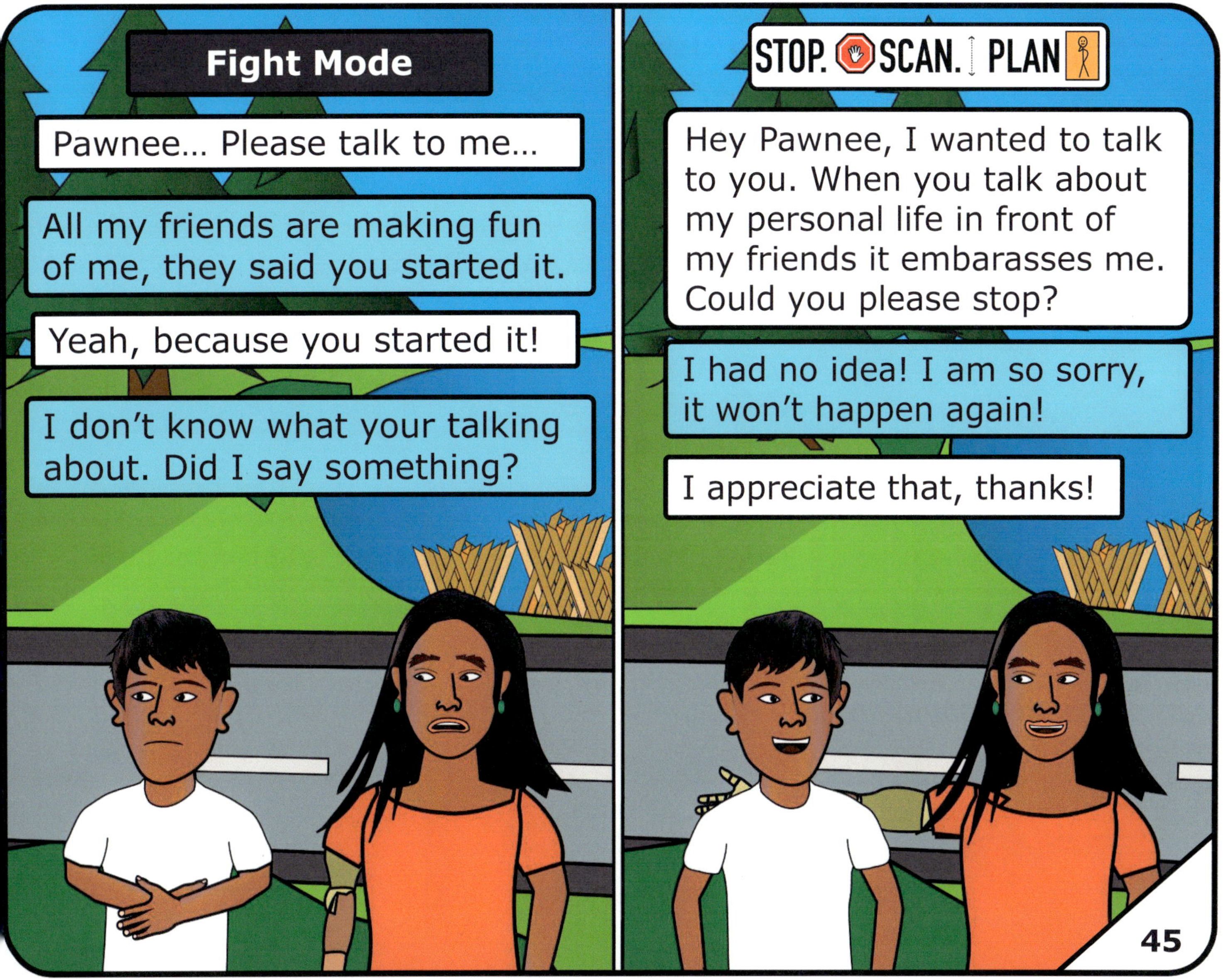
Fight Mode
Pawnee… Please talk to me…
All my friends are making fun of me, they said you started it.
Yeah, because you started it!
I don't know what your talking about. Did I say something?
STOP. SCAN. PLAN
Hey Pawnee, I wanted to talk to you. When you talk about my personal life in front of my friends it embarasses me. Could you please stop?
I had no idea! I am so sorry, it won't happen again!
I appreciate that, thanks!

Let's try this now by guiding Rishi.

Situation: Rishi is going on his first rollercoaster ride. He is getting very scared and considering leaving the line. He has heard it is fun though...

His Thoughts

I have been really looking forward to going on Space Coaster, but now I'm scared! Could I die???

His Feelings

Excited, **anxious**, worried, terrified.

The Moment of Choice!

STOP. SCAN. PLAN

Stop! Box Breath
☐ 1...2...3...4...

Use the TFB in Me!
Thoughts? Feelings? Facts?
What can he control? Options?

What should he do?	How will this make him feel? Why?

Help Frankie with this money choice!

Situation: Frankie is shoe shopping.
He has $200. He has wanted one pair for the longest time, but those shoes are very expensive.
What should he do?

His Thoughts

I have been really looking forward to going on Space Coaster, but now I'm scared!
Could I die???

His Feelings

Unsure, nervous, excited.

The Moment of Choice!

STOP. SCAN. PLAN

Stop! Box Breath
☐ 1...2...3...4...

Use the TFB in Me!
Thoughts? Feelings? Facts?
What can he control? Options?

What should he do?

How will this make him feel? Why?

Using the TFB in Me is a tool for handling the risk and stress in your life!
Thoughts
Feelings
TFB
Behaviors
STOP. SCAN. PLAN

Step 2:
Understand how thoughts, feelings and behaviors are connected.

Now it is your turn! Think of a situation where you could map out your thoughts, feelings and behaviors!

What was the risk or situation?

What were you thinking?

How did you feel?

What did you do?

How to Handle Risk!

Our next goal is to take what we have learned with your **TFB (Thoughts, Feelings and Behaviors)** and apply that to our choices with **personal finances!**

So how do we handle the risks that we encounter financially? **By planning ahead!** Just like we have set our course to see our friend Evelyn at the Insurance Agency.

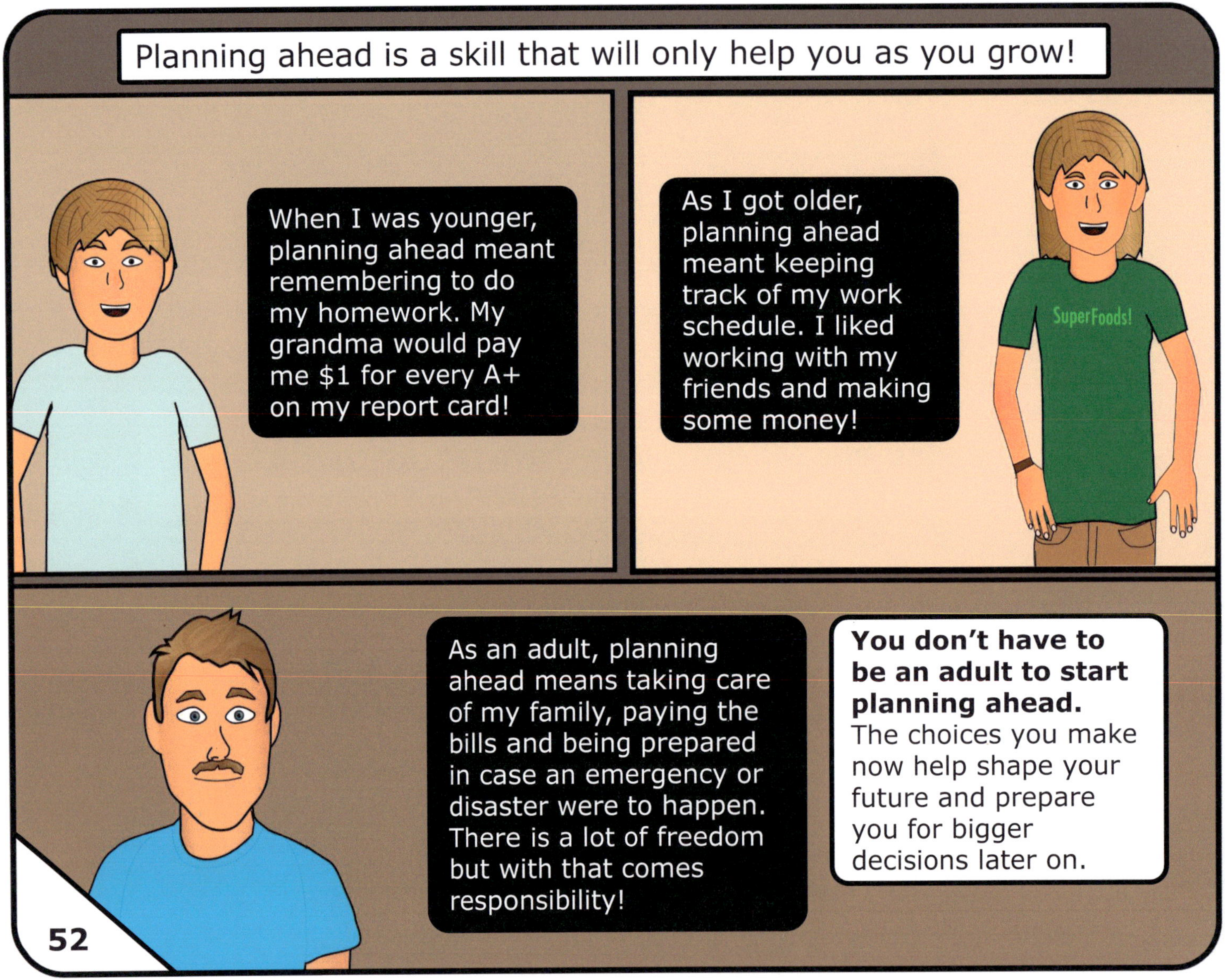

Planning ahead is a skill that will only help you as you grow!
When I was younger, planning ahead meant remembering to do my homework. My grandma would pay me $1 for every A+ on my report card!
As I got older, planning ahead meant keeping track of my work schedule. I liked working with my friends and making some money!
SuperFoods!
As an adult, planning ahead means taking care of my family, paying the bills and being prepared in case an emergency or disaster were to happen. There is a lot of freedom but with that comes responsibility!
You don't have to be an adult to start planning ahead. The choices you make now help shape your future and prepare you for bigger decisions later on.

Planning ahead helps you become more independent!

Planning ahead helps reduce stress and gives you more control over your choices. Here are some example of how you could plan ahead:

- Turn in homework early
- Study before screen time
- Do your chores
- Stick to your routine
- Stay calm when upset
- Walk away from drama
- Put your phone away
- Think before you speak
- Save money for later

Which of these do you feel like you do a good job at already? Explain why for each!

Pick one of these you feel like you could do a better job at? What could you do to improve?

We need some STARR power! When it comes to risk we have to consider the different ways of handling it!

Different situations may call for different methods. We can **share**, **transfer**, **avoid**, **retain** or **reduce**. To help remember this we use the acronym **STARR**!

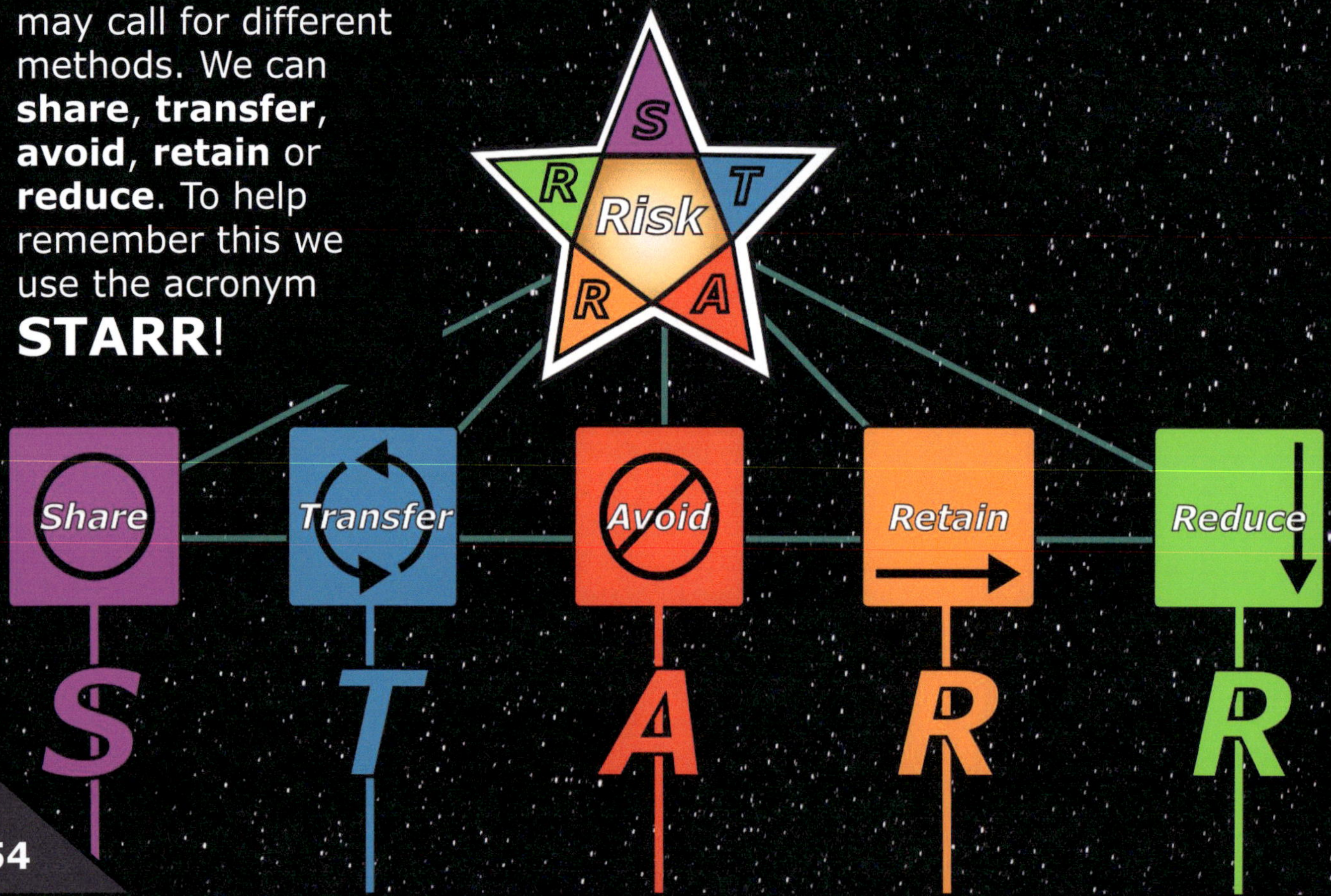

When it comes to risk there is no perfect way to handle it. It can be helpful to consider the **costs and the benefits**. Some people call this "pros and cons."

Cost and Benefits:
A system where you compare the positive and negative consequences of a choice.

Key Word

Benefits (pros)	Costs (cons)
How will this help me?	**What will this require of me?**

Let's take a look at each of the ways of handling risk!

Share

Sharing Risk:

When you take on risk with another person or group.

For example, if a person is planning a party with a group of friends, each person is taking on part of the risk!

Tim works for the postal service, helping deliver mail across an entire city with his team. Sometimes he runs behind, maybe due to traffic or stopping to help an elderly person. When that happens, he can call a teammate to cover the route so everyone still gets their mail and the job gets done! Together they make work better!

Sharing risk is a great way to build trust and strengthen friendships. However, it comes with it's own risk, **can you rely on others?**

Benefits	Costs
• You each bring different strengths. • You share the costs and spreads out the effort. • Safety in numbers!	• You have to share control with others. • When others make mistakes you share responsibility and the consequences.

Scenario:
You are planning a party with your 3 best friends.
Each person takes on different tasks and shares the costs.
Share each person's role and what they would do:

Transfer Risk:
When you are able to give someone else your risk.

For example, when a person adopts a pet they are taking the risk of the pet, a transfer of responsibility.

Kristen works for the news station as a reporter. She's been doing this for years and has built some really great relationships. She's given an assignment to interview the owner of a coffee shop... problem is, it's her ex-boyfriend. She asks a friend to take it instead so she can avoid an awkward encounter.

Transferring risk can quickly remove the pressure of stress. However, it also means you are no longer involved. **Are you willing to give it up?**

Benefits	Costs
• You will no longer be the one responsible. • Someone might handle it better than you.	• You likely will lose money or the option by giving it to another person. • You lose control of that risk.

Scenario:
Your mom wants to give you more time for reading and decides to give your siblings one of your chores. Which chore would you give them? Why?

Avoid Risk:
When you find ways to not experience the risk.

For example, if a person is scared of sharks they won't swim in the ocean.

Amir is a doctor, and he helps people with all kinds of problems. He's seen things no one wants to see in the emergency room. It's a hard job, but helping others brings him joy. His brother loves motorcycles and invites him on a cross-country trip. Amir says no, riding a motorcycle feels way too dangerous to him.

Avoiding Risk is an effective way to keep yourself safe. However, it also comes with the cost of experience. **Will you regret missing out?**

Benefits	Costs
• Avoiding helps you to know you are safe from the risk, physically or financially. • It's a way to stay away from harm!	• You can miss out on opportunities that could have been really good. • You might become afraid to try things.

Scenario:
Everyone has different tastes when it comes to food.
One person may love onions, whereas another may hate them.
Are there any foods that you try to avoid? Give examples!

Retain →

Retain Risk:

When you recognize the risk and choose not to change it

For example, if a person plays a sport they know they could get hurt, yet they still do it.

Ana works at the police station. Sometimes this means going out into the city and following up on 911 calls. She just got a call about a family that came home and their door was open. She goes to the address and meets the family outside. She holsters her weapon and enters the house. Thankfully everything was okay.

Retaining risk is a part of life, we have to take risks! However, there are times when we should be more careful. **Act or wait and plan?**

Benefits	Costs
• You are in control and it can help you build your self confidence to do things safely.	• You are exposed to risk and it could be stressful. • It could lead to a loss of money or options.

Scenario:
When making a purchase you are taking a risk.
Can you think of a time when you spent money and wish you had saved it instead? Share the situation:

Reduce Risk:
When you find and use ways to make the risk less.

For example, a person riding a bike wears a helmet for safety.
A house has cameras to prevent theft.

Jack is a high school student who wants to start investing early. He works at a local fast food place and plans to buy mutual funds when he turns eighteen. Realizing he has a lot to learn, he asks the Personal Finance teacher to mentor him. Together they agree to meet weekly and discuss different ways of investing.

Reducing risk let's us get to do the things we want while being safe. However, this takes time and often resources. **Worth it?**

Benefits	Costs
• You can make the risk less dangerous and open up more opportunities! • Recognize + Reduce = Relax!	• You might spend time, money and energy to reduce risk and then later realize it didn't work.

Scenario:
You and your family are going on a vacation in the woods. The trip is a two hour drive and you will be there three days. What can you do to prepare for your trip and make it safer?

Use STARR power when faced with risk!
S T A R R
Risk
How would you handle each of these risks?
TOBACCO
Being offered tobacco!
Homework!
Finishing homework!
Skateboarding!
100
2021
Buying headphones!
Feeling depressed.

Answer these questions about how **STARR** can help you make decisions in your everyday life!

How could you **sharing** work on a big school project to make it less stressful?

Is there a task you could **give to someone else** to help reduce your stress?

Have you ever **avoided** a risky or uncomfortable situation? What helped you decide?

Share a time when you knew there was some risk involved and **you did it anyway?**

What's something you could do to make a situation feel **safer or less stressful?**

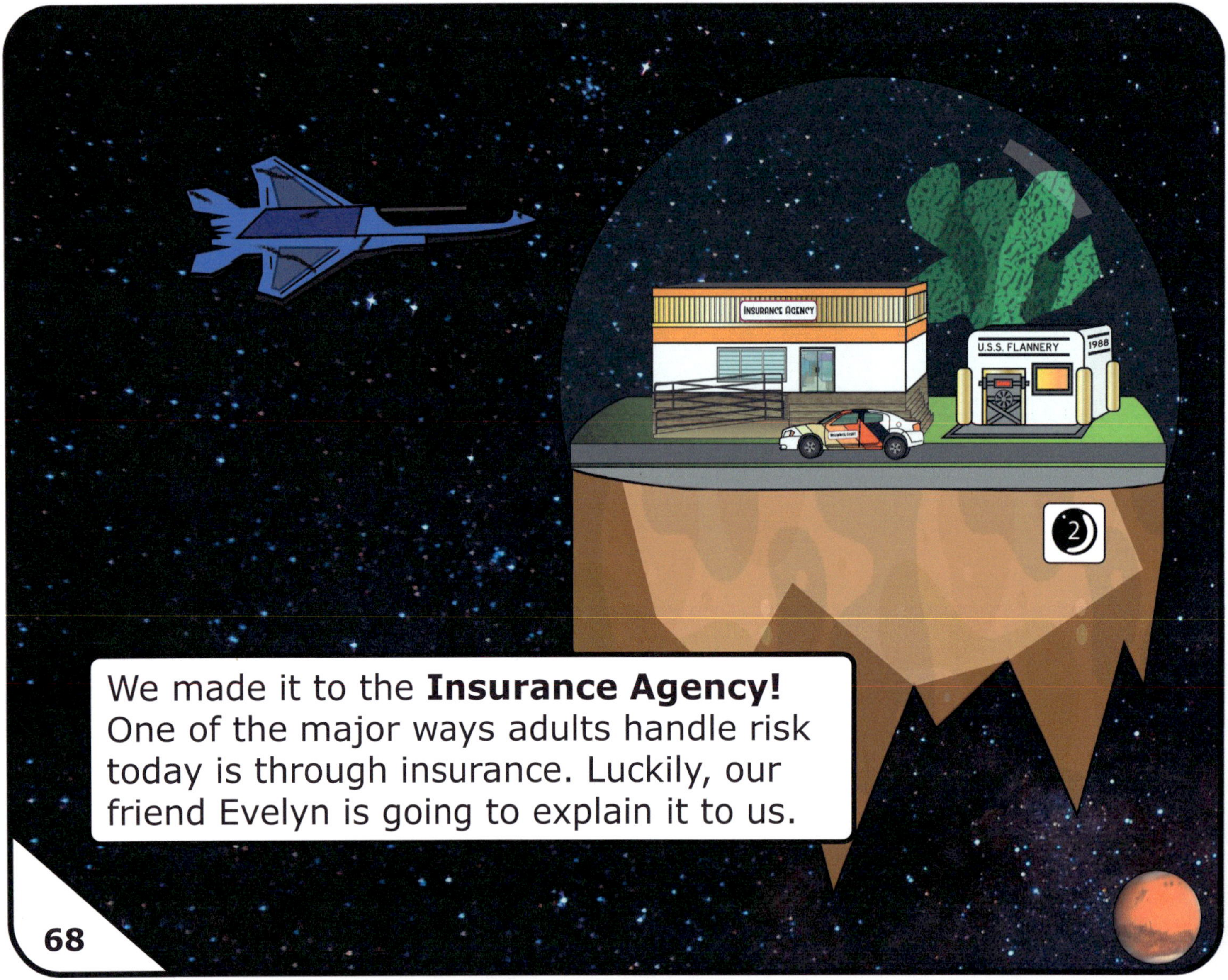

We made it to the **Insurance Agency!** One of the major ways adults handle risk today is through insurance. Luckily, our friend Evelyn is going to explain it to us.

Hey Mr. GreatCents! Hey DT-7G! I have been looking forward to our meeting, how was your trip?
Hey Evelyn! So glad we made it. We ran into a domino cluster and I was worried we wouldn't make it.
INSURANCE AGENCY
Beep-Beep!
U.S.S.
Is your ship okay? If not, we have you covered. Let's take a look at it really quick.

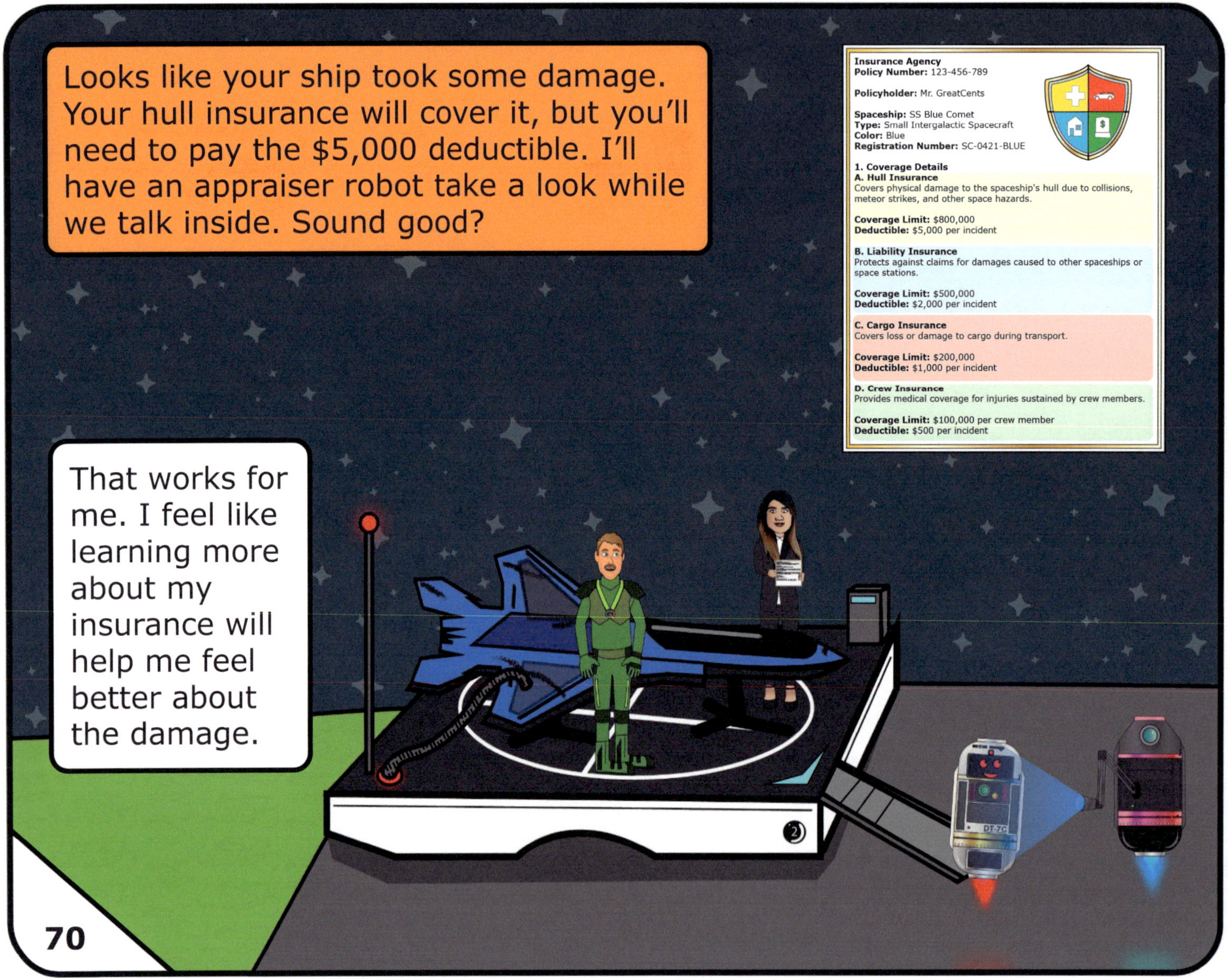
Looks like your ship took some damage. Your hull insurance will cover it, but you'll need to pay the $5,000 deductible. I'll have an appraiser robot take a look while we talk inside. Sound good?
Insurance Agency
Policy Number: 123-456-789
Policyholder: Mr. GreatCents
Spaceship: SS Blue Comet
Type: Small Intergalactic Spacecraft
Color: Blue
Registration Number: SC-0421-BLUE
1. Coverage Details
A. Hull Insurance
Covers physical damage to the spaceship's hull due to collisions, meteor strikes, and other space hazards.
Coverage Limit: $800,000
Deductible: $5,000 per incident
B. Liability Insurance
Protects against claims for damages caused to other spaceships or space stations.
Coverage Limit: $500,000
Deductible: $2,000 per incident
C. Cargo Insurance
Covers loss or damage to cargo during transport.
Coverage Limit: $200,000
Deductible: $1,000 per incident
D. Crew Insurance
Provides medical coverage for injuries sustained by crew members.
Coverage Limit: $100,000 per crew member
Deductible: $500 per incident
That works for me. I feel like learning more about my insurance will help me feel better about the damage.
DT-7C

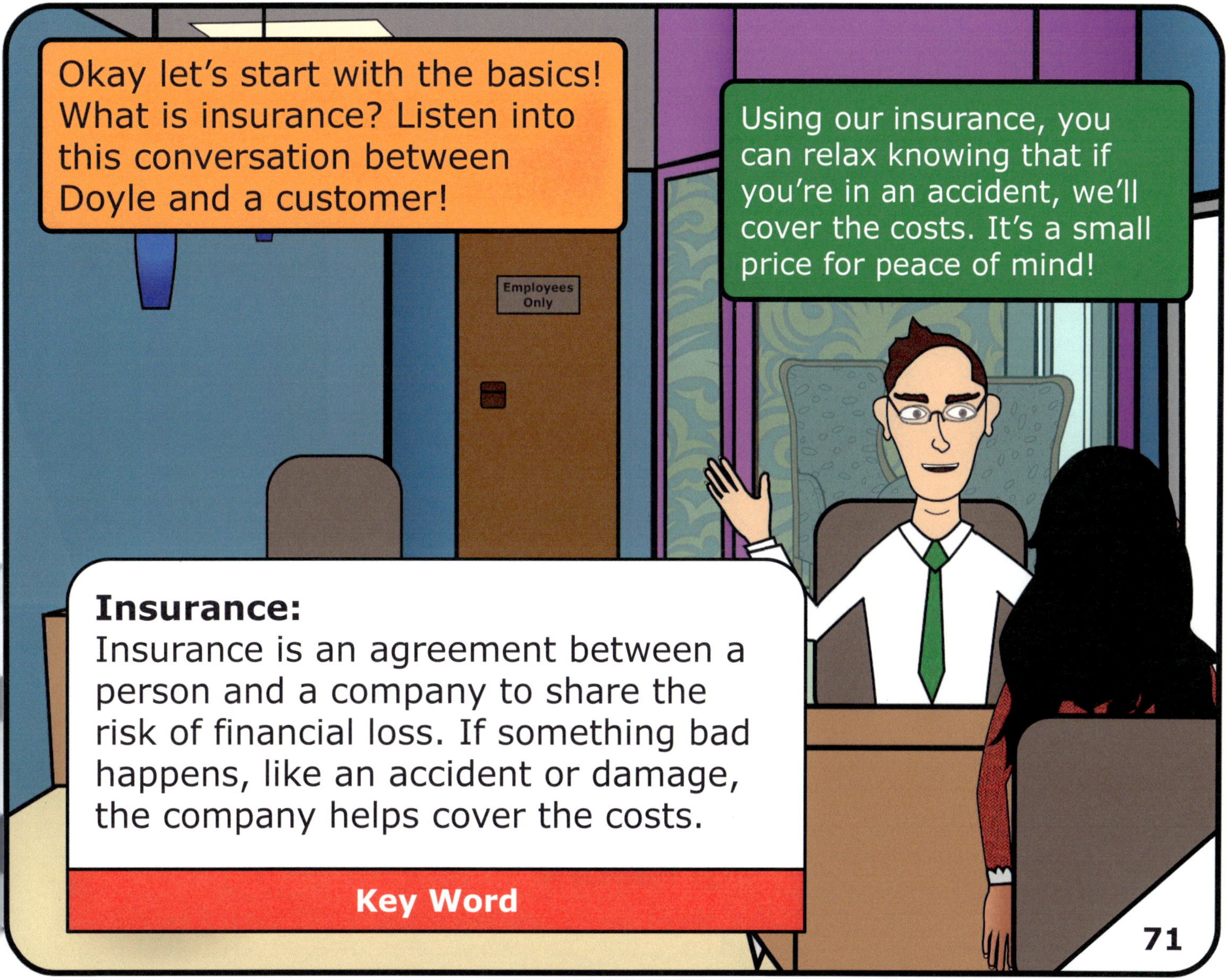
Okay let's start with the basics! What is insurance? Listen into this conversation between Doyle and a customer!
Using our insurance, you can relax knowing that if you're in an accident, we'll cover the costs. It's a small price for peace of mind!
Employees Only
Insurance:
Insurance is an agreement between a person and a company to share the risk of financial loss. If something bad happens, like an accident or damage, the company helps cover the costs.
Key Word

You are also required to have certain types of insurance by law. When sitting with an agent, they will share what they can provide. Make sure your insurance fits your situation, if you don't have a pet, don't get insurance for it!

Here are some of our products. If you get your home and auto insurance through us we can buncle it and give you a big discount.

What we can cover:

Health Insurance
Definition: Helps cover medical expenses when you visit doctors, ge
prescriptions, or need hospital care.
Required: Yes, in many places it is required to have health insuranc
a penalty.

Auto Insurance
Definition: Provides financial protection for damages or injuries caused b
car accident. It can also cover theft or damage to your car.
Required: Yes, auto insurance is legally required in most places if you own a vehicle.

Home/Renters Insurance
Definition: Covers damage to your home or belongings, and may also provide liability protection if someone is injured on your property.
Required: No, but it is highly recommended. If you own a home with a mortgage, your lender will likely require it.

Life Insurance
Definition: Pays money to your beneficiaries (like family) if you pass away, helping them cover expenses and maintain financial stability.
Required: No, but it is recommended for those who want to provide financial support to loved ones after they are gone.

Pet Insurance
Definition: Helps cover veterinary costs for your pet's illnesses or injuries.
Required: No, but it is recommended for pet owners to help manage unexpected medical expenses.

Phone Insurance
Definition: Covers repairs or replacement of your phone if it is damaged, lost, or stolen.
Required: No, but it can be useful if you want protection for your phone.

Plane Insurance
Definition: Covers damages or loss related to private aircraft or commercial flight. This can include damage to the plane or liability for accidents.
Required: No, but it is required for private plane owners and can be optional for travelers.

Umbrella Insurance
Definition: Provides extra coverage beyond your standard insurance policies (like auto or home) to protect against large claims or lawsuits.
Required: No, but it is recommended for additional financial protection.

Step 3: Identify the ways a person can handle risk personally and financially.

Beep-Beep!

Who is someone that handles risk well?

Share a situation where you feel like this person did a good job of handling the risk? What did they do?

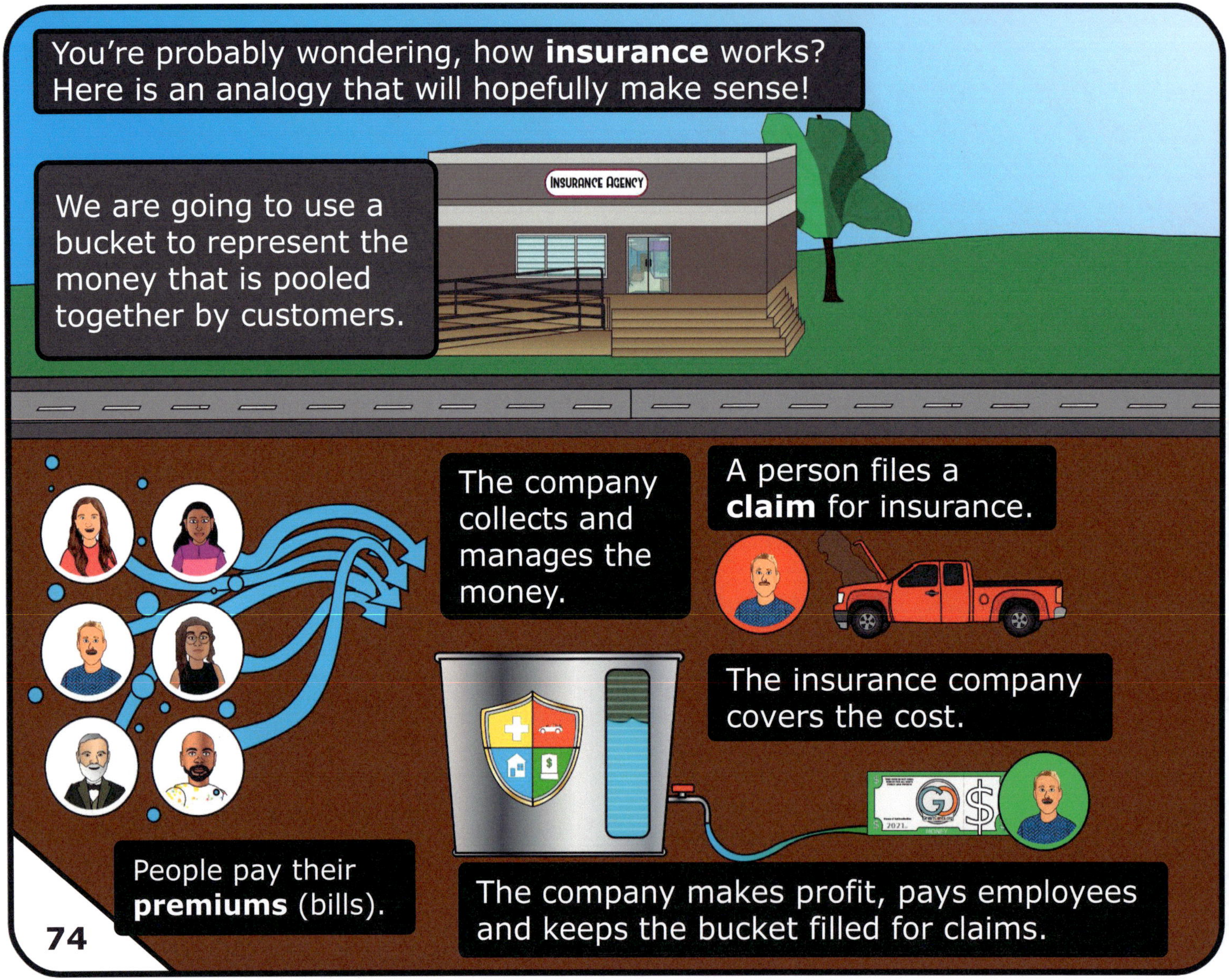

You're probably wondering, how **insurance** works? Here is an analogy that will hopefully make sense!
We are going to use a bucket to represent the money that is pooled together by customers.
INSURANCE AGENCY
The company collects and manages the money.
A person files a **claim** for insurance.
The insurance company covers the cost.
People pay their **premiums** (bills).
The company makes profit, pays employees and keeps the bucket filled for claims.

Another way of thinking about **insurance** is as a safety net. Life is filled with risk, like working on a tall building, if you fall off do you want something to catch you?

How would having a safety net help you to work as a construction worker?

How would having insurance help you to make choices as a person?

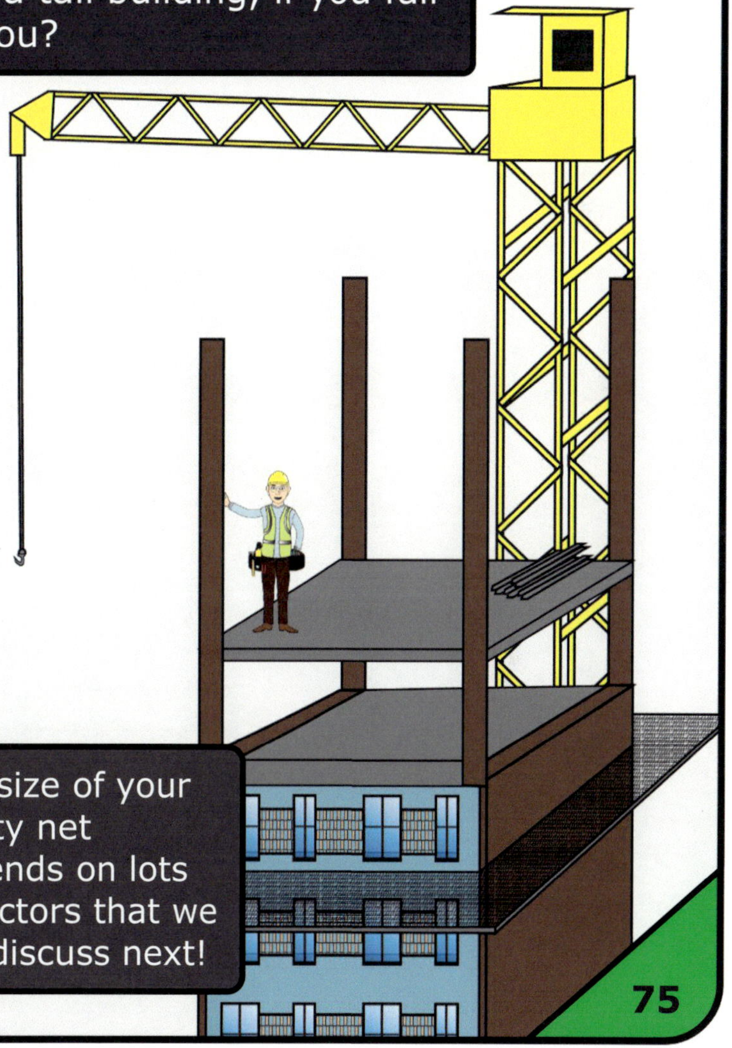

The size of your safety net depends on lots of factors that we will discuss next!

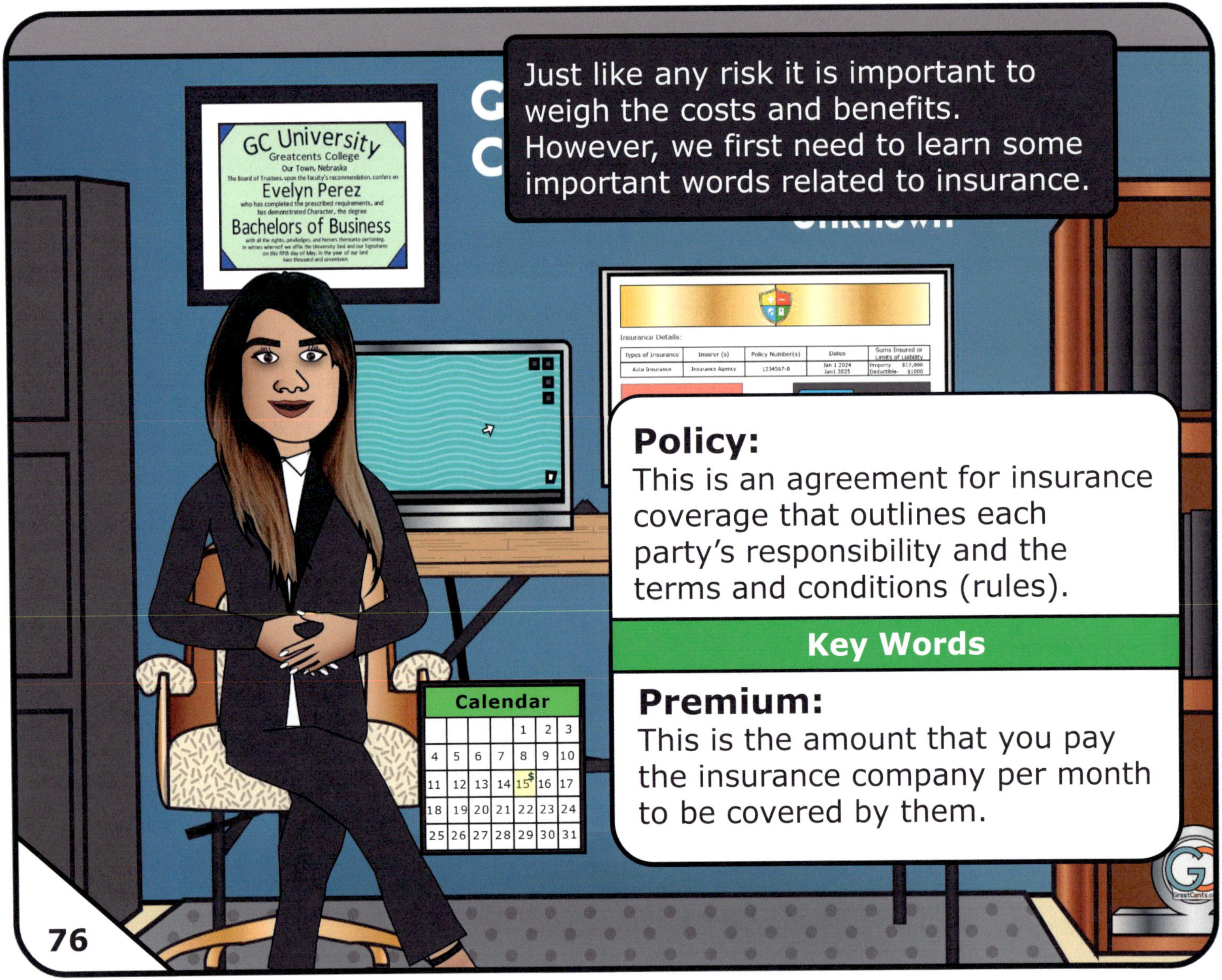
GC University
Greatcents College
Our Town, Nebraska
Evelyn Perez
Bachelors of Business
Just like any risk it is important to weigh the costs and benefits. However, we first need to learn some important words related to insurance.
Insurance Details:
Calendar
Policy:
This is an agreement for insurance coverage that outlines each party's responsibility and the terms and conditions (rules).
Key Words
Premium:
This is the amount that you pay the insurance company per month to be covered by them.

What is an agreement?
How does it work?

When you are signing up for insurance, you are likely to hear a lot of terms that you might not be familiar with. **Slow down and make sure you understand what you are agreeing to before signing a policy.**

Once signed they will charge you! Here are some payment options!

Time	Monthly	Quarterly	Semiannually	Annually
How long between payments?				
Examples:	Health Insurance **$350**	Health Insurance **$1,020**	Health Insurance **$2,000**	Health Insurance **$3,900**
Cost at payment	$	$$$	$$$$$	$$$$$$$

If your premium feels overwhelming, meaning too expensive, there is a way to lower your monthly cost

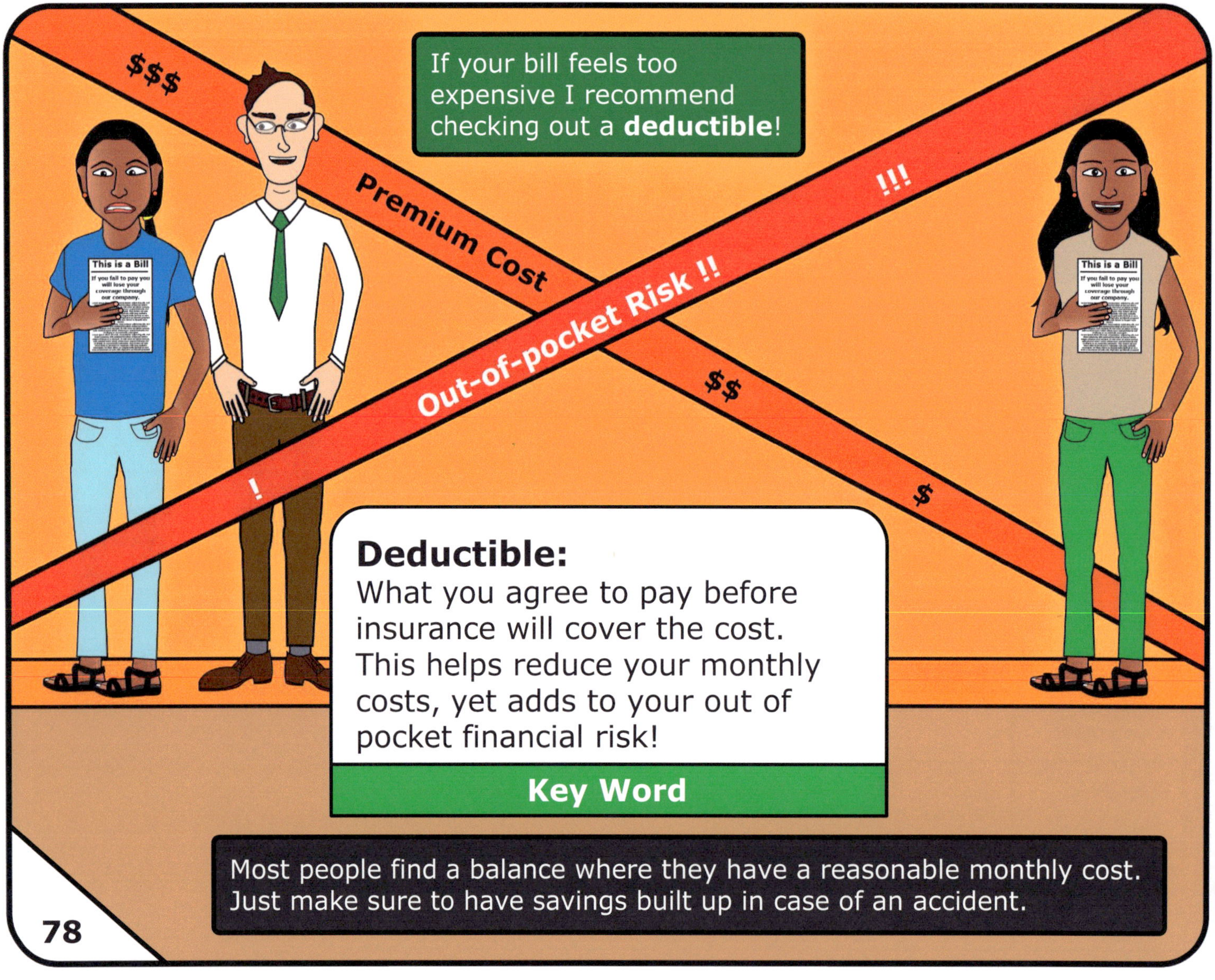
If your bill feels too expensive I recommend checking out a **deductible**!
$$$
Premium Cost
$$
$
!!!
Out-of-pocket Risk !!
!
This is a Bill
If you fail to pay you will lose your coverage through our company.
This is a Bill
If you fail to pay you will lose your coverage through our company.
Deductible:
What you agree to pay before insurance will cover the cost. This helps reduce your monthly costs, yet adds to your out of pocket financial risk!
Key Word
Most people find a balance where they have a reasonable monthly cost. Just make sure to have savings built up in case of an accident.

Figuring out your preferred insurance cost is a bit of a dance!
Who is going to take the lead and take more risk. A great driver could save thousands of dollars each year by taking a larger deductible.

Premium	Deductible	Yearly cost no accidents
Payment **$200** Monthly	**None**	**$2,400**
Payment **$150** Monthly	**Small** One Time $250	**$1,800**
Payment **$110** Monthly	**Medium** One Time $500	**$1,320**
Payment **$70** Monthly	**Large** One Time $1000	**$840**

Which deductible do you think fits your level of risk? Why?

So if I have an accident then the insurance company will pay for everything to be fixed?

Not quite, it will depend on your **coverage**.

Coverage:
The specific events, situations, or types of damage that your insurance policy will pay for.

Key Word

Pet Insurance Policy Agreement

Policyholder Information:
Name: Badeea
Address: Our Town
Phone: 308-888-8888
Email: Badeea@greatcents.org

Pet Information:
Pet Name: Whiskers
Species: Cat
Breed: American Shorthair
Date of Birth: March 24th

Insurance Coverage:
This policy provides coverage for the following:
Veterinary care due to illness or injury
Prescription medications
Diagnostic tests
Surgical procedures
Emergency care
Specialist consultations

Exclusions:
The following are not covered under this policy:
Routine wellness exams
Vaccinations
Spaying/neutering
Pre-existing conditions
Dental care (unless related to an accident)
Grooming services, including haircuts, nail trims, and bathing
Behavioral therapy
Breeding, pregnancy, or giving birth

Policy Terms:
Deductible: $500 per incident
Reimbursement Rate: 80%
Annual Limit: $10,000
Premium: $30 per month

Fine Print:
All claims are subject to review and approval by the insurance provider. Policyholders are responsible for any costs incurred that are not covered by this policy.

Policyholder Acknowledgment:
I, Badeea, acknowledge that I have read and understand the terms and conditions of this pet insurance policy. I agree to abide by the exclusions and limitations outlined above, including the exclusion of grooming services.

Signature: Badeea
Date: July 30th 2024

For example: pet insurance is likely to cover medical costs if your pet is hurt, but it won't cover getting your cat a haircut.

That is why you have to check the fine print! Insurance companies will only do what they agreed to do.

Insurance may sound great, but you need to read the fine print before it is too late! Below are several things covered by phone insurance.

Why would phone insurance cover theft, but not losing your phone?

With health insurance some doctors will be covered and others won't (out of network).

If you were hurt or sick where would you go for help?

Once you have insurance you can relax… until something happens that is covered by insurance. Then you need to make a **claim**.

Claim:
A request you make to your insurance company to help pay for costs after something covered by your policy happen, like an accident or damage.

Key Word

There are many ways to file a **claim**: online, through a mobile app, by phone call, via email, or through an agent. If you are paying for insurance, it is worth using it!

Lastly, a person called an **insurance appraiser** will come and check the claim. They will be inspecting the damage, gathering information and creating an estimate of what the damage is worth. Right now I'm downloading the data on your ship.
www.insuranceagency-galaxy.com/reports/bluecomet2024
Damage Valuation Report
Spaceship: SS Blue Comet
Policyholder: Mr. GreatCents
Inspection Date: Stardate 2024.07.25
Damage Inspector: Alex Nova
1. Overview
The SS Blue Comet experienced damage during an incident involving a collision with a small asteroid field. This report provides a detailed assessment of the damages and estimated repair costs.
2. Inspection Findings
A. Hull Damage
Location: Port side, mid-section
Extent: 30% of the port side hull surface has dents and punctures. Several structural beams are bent.
Repair Estimate: $250,000
Description: The impacted area requires replacement of damaged panels, realignment of structural beams, and re-sealing to ensure hull integrity.
B. Engine System
Location: Main engine compartment
Extent: Minor cosmetic damage with no impact on functionality.
Repair Estimate: $5,000
Description: Minor repairs include cosmetic touch-ups and a thorough inspection to ensure no internal damage.
C. Cargo Bay
Location: Rear cargo bay
Extent: Minor misalignment of cargo bay doors, no damage to contents.
Repair Estimate: $10,000
Description: The doors require minor realignment and recalibration of the locking mechanism.
D. Interior Systems
Location: Various (life support, navigation)
Extent: Minor adjustments needed to recalibrate systems.
Repair Estimate: $5,000
Description: Minor recalibrations to ensure optimal performance of life support and navigation systems.
3. Total Estimated Repair Cost
Total Estimate: $270,000
4. Additional Notes
Timeframe for Repairs: Estimated at 3-4 weeks, depending on parts availability and repair facility capacity.
Potential Downtime Costs: Not included in this estimate; to be calculated based on lost mission time or revenue.
Report Prepared by:
Appraiser Bot 3
Title: Damage Inspector
Signature:
For: Insurance Agency
Date: Stardate 2024.07.25
If everything checks out, the insurance company will send you the funds you are owed.

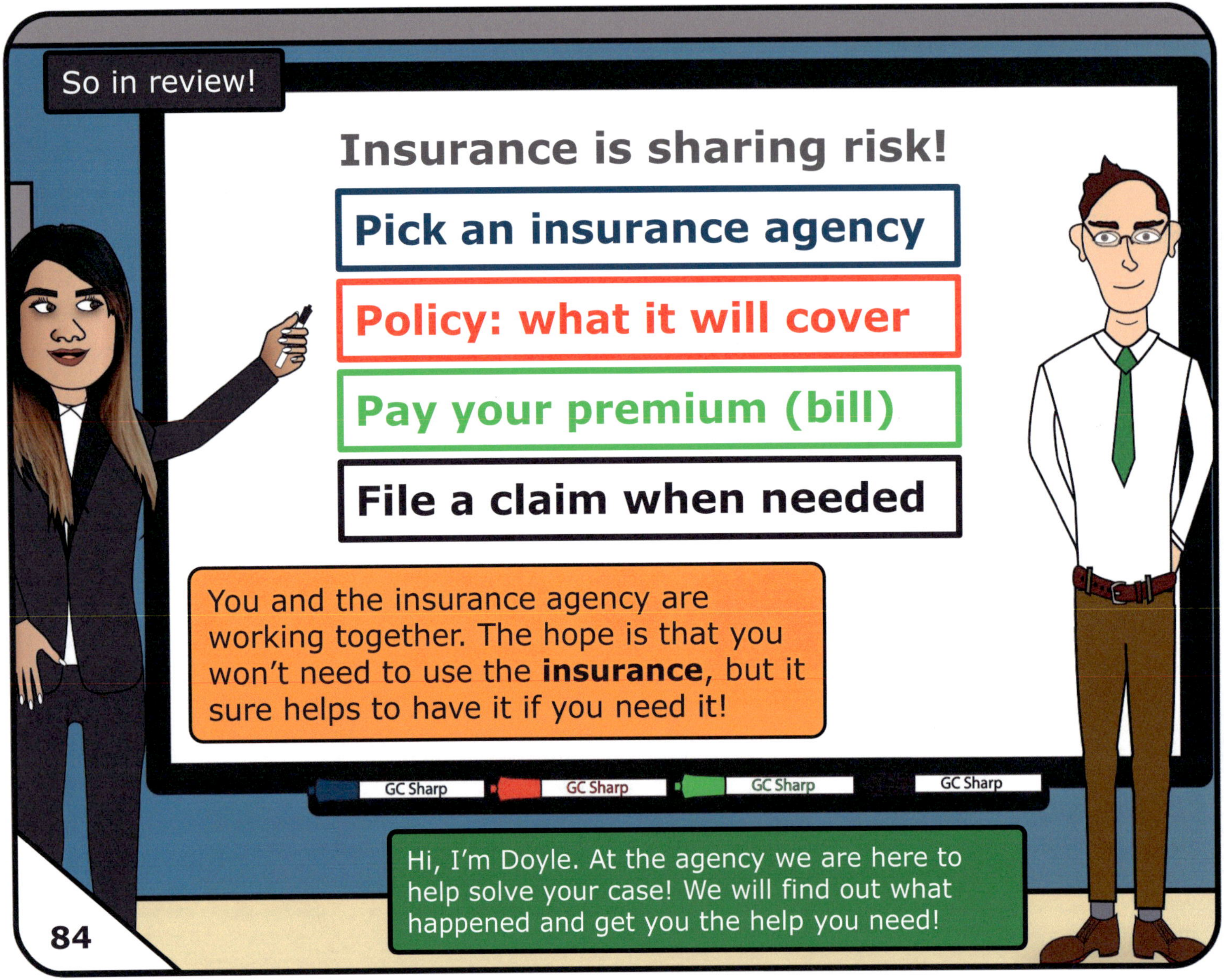

So in review!
Insurance is sharing risk!
Pick an insurance agency
Policy: what it will cover
Pay your premium (bill)
File a claim when needed
You and the insurance agency are working together. The hope is that you won't need to use the **insurance**, but it sure helps to have it if you need it!
GC Sharp
GC Sharp
GC Sharp
GC Sharp
Hi, I'm Doyle. At the agency we are here to help solve your case! We will find out what happened and get you the help you need!

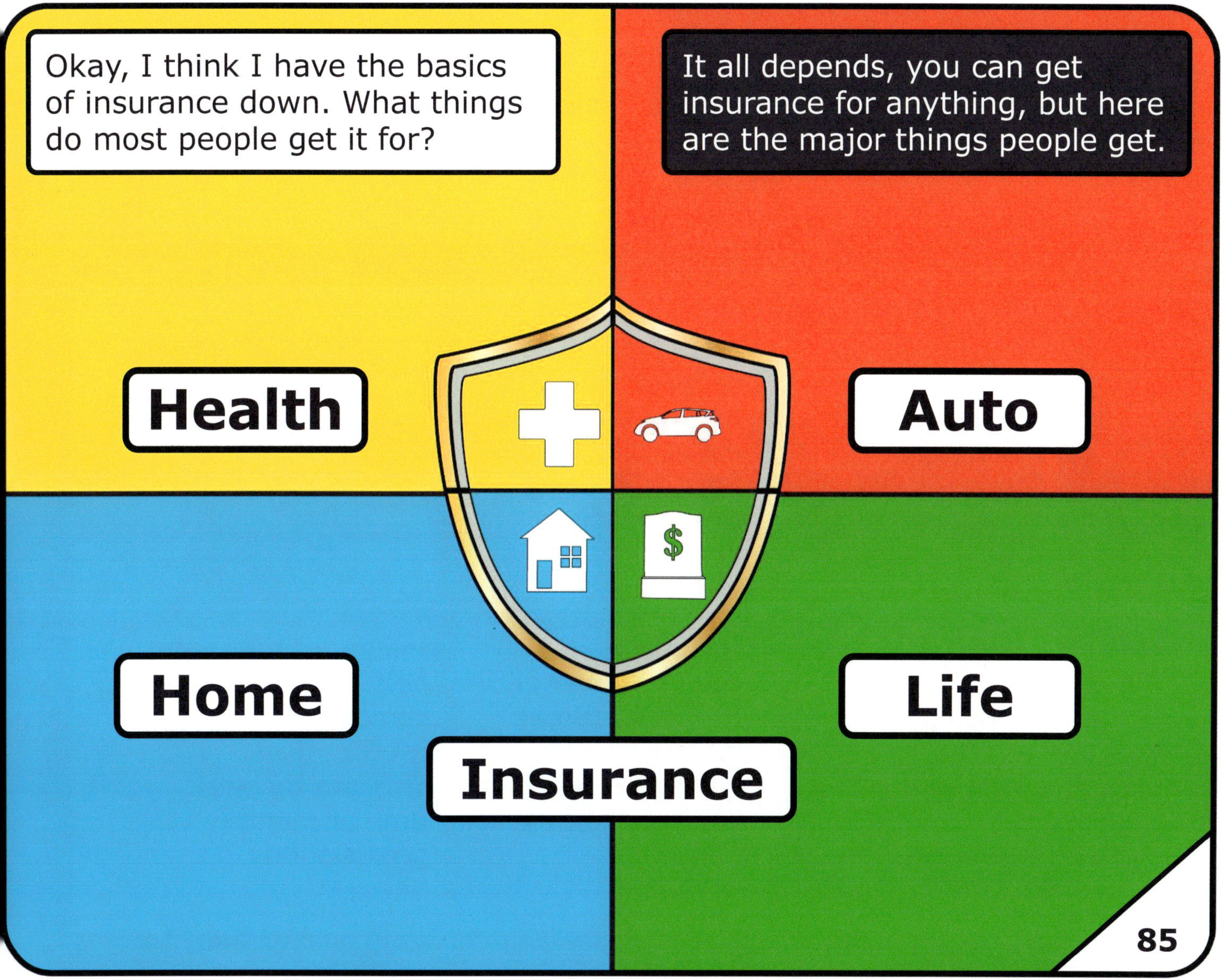
Okay, I think I have the basics of insurance down. What things do most people get it for?
It all depends, you can get insurance for anything, but here are the major things people get.
Health
Auto
Home
Life
$
Insurance

Have you ever had to go to the doctor or get medicine?

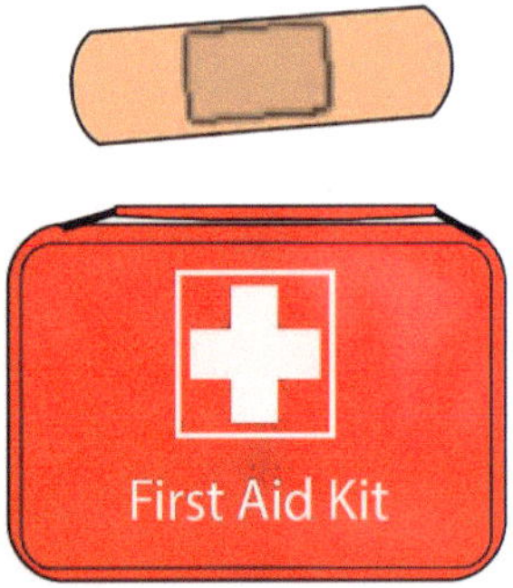

Insurance helps cover check ups, which help you to maintaining good health. They call it **preventative care.**

Health Insurance: This is a type of insurance that covers the costs related to medical needs and emergencies.

Key Word

Insurance also covers **minor** and **major medical emergencies.** Medical costs can build up quickly!

Insurance also can help cover cost that comes with **medication.** This can be one time or monthly prescriptions.

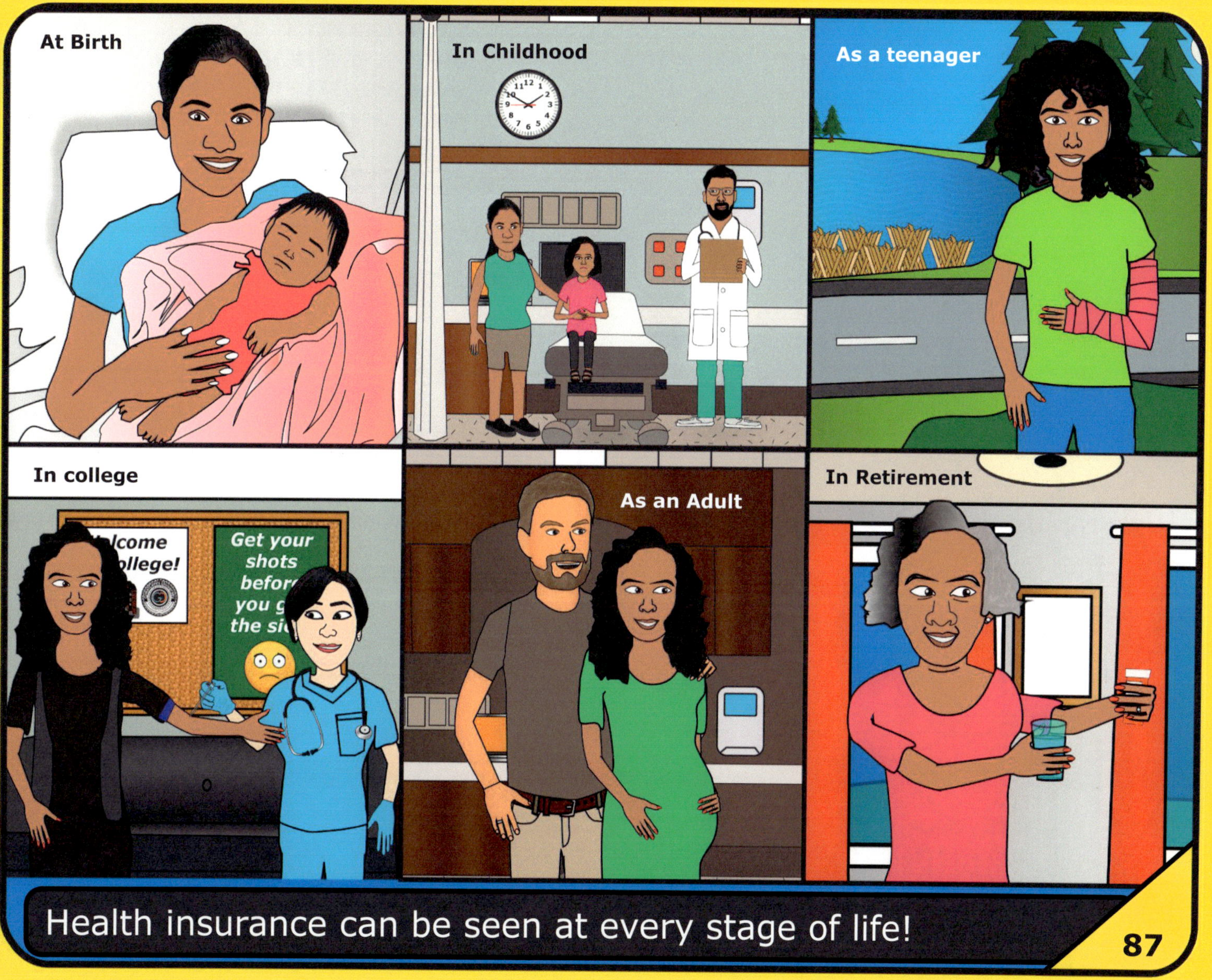

At Birth
In Childhood
As a teenager
In college
Get your
shots
As an Adult
In Retirement
Health insurance can be seen at every stage of life!

With **health insurance** they want to make **preventative care** a priority. The best way to save money with sickness and injuries is to keep it from happening! **Share ways that you can protect parts of your body!**

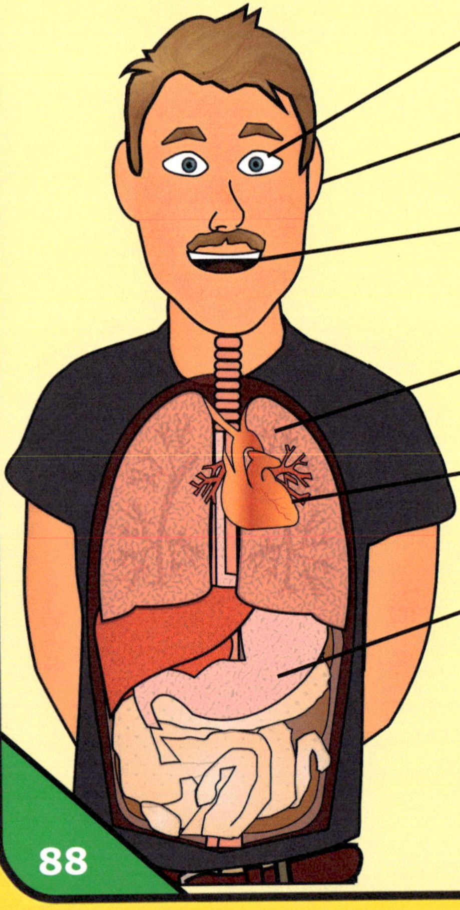

Eyes	
Ears	
Teeth	
Lungs	
Heart	
Gut	

Self-management is key to living a healthy life! You only get one body in life and it's so important to build great habits and take care of your mind. Stress messes with your body!

Medicine is an important part of health care. A person can take medication (**drugs**) through pills, creams, drinks and many other ways! It is important to consider the **costs** and **benefits** whenever taking any type of medication.

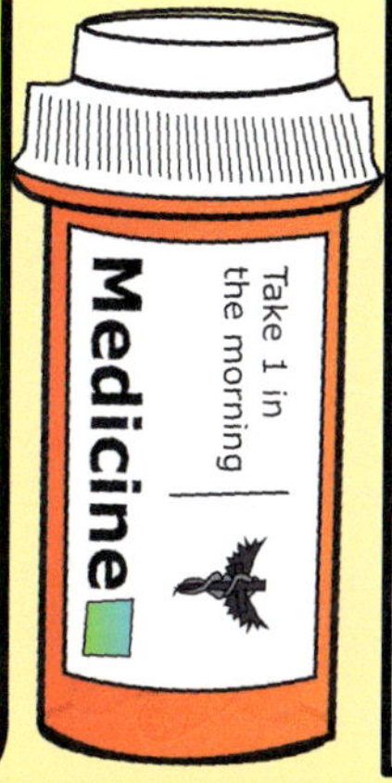

Share an example of a time a person might take medication?

So when is something considered a major medical emergency?
Here is a list of reasons to seek medical help from professionals.

Bleeding that won't stop	**Broken bone** or dislocated joint	**Chest pain** or tightness	**Fainting** or passing out
Head injury with confusion or passing out	**High fever** with stiff neck or rash	**Poisoning** or taking too much medicine	**Head, neck, or spine** injuries
Really bad **headache**	**Seizures**	Serious **burns**	**Trouble breathing**

What phone number do you call in the case of an medical emergency?

How many vehicle have you rode in this past week? Why?

Everyone driving is required by law to have insurance. When students are able to drive they can be added on their parent's insurance.

Why is it required? A person shouldn't have to pay for an accident that someone else caused. Insurance covers these costs.

Important: There are several levels of car insurance. **Each person has the right to get what fits their needs.**

Car Insurance: This is insurance that covers cost related to car accidents and other damage to your car.

Key Word

Liability Insurance:
This covers the debt a person would owe for damage to a person's property and injuries.

The more that insurance covers the more it will cost.

Collision Insurance:
This covers the cost of repair for your vehicle in the case that you hit another car or object that causes damage.

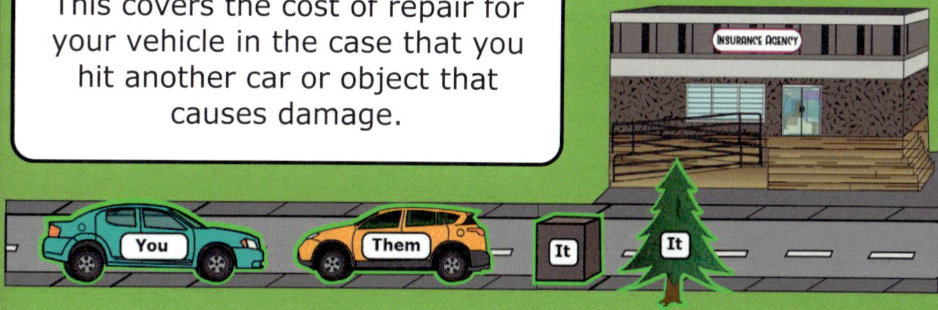

Comprehensive Insurance:
This covers most things that could harm your vehicle other than a collision.
For example:
• storm damage (hail, wind, floods, lightning, hurricanes, earthquakes),
• theft • vandalism • fire • falling objects
• windshield damage • animal damage
• other unexpected damage.

Everyone makes mistakes at times. When it comes to car accidents it can be very expensive. This is why there are different parts of **liability insurance**!

Property damage liability covers the cost related to buildings or cars getting repaired.

Why might someone crash into a building or fence? Give several reasons!

Bodily injury liability covers the cost related to any medical bills for people hurt in the accident.

Why should a person wear a seat belt when driving or riding in their vehicle?

Do you like your car? Having **collision insurance** can give you the comfort of knowing your car could be replaced in the case of an accident.

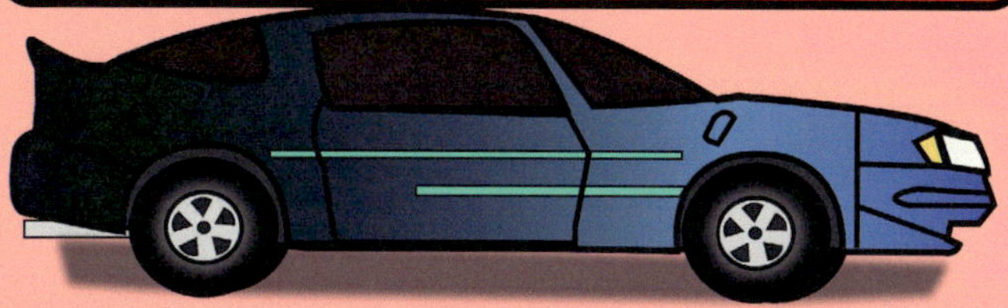

Comprehensive Insurance covers the many unexpected things that could harm your vehicle.

Score these potential dangers by **how likely they are to happen where you live:** 1 low - 10 high →

Have you ever seen or heard of a car accident? What happened?

How much does a new car cost? If you buy a new car with a loan you have to have collision insurance, why?

	Theft	Someone steals your car
	Vandalism	Someone breaks your window
	Fire damage	A forest fire
	Weather damage	A tornado or hailstorm
	Flood damage	Water ruins your car
	Falling objects	A falling tree branch or rock
	Hitting an animal	A deer gets hit by your car
	Glass damage	A rock cracks your windshield

What is your home like? Have you ever seen storm damage?

A person gets **Renters insurance** if they are renting where they live. The landlord covers the insurance for the building. **Very affordable.**

This covers:
Personal Property (repairing or replacing your belongings),
Liability - money you owe for repairs. (accidental injuries and property damage)
Living Expenses (costs if you can't live where you are renting).

Home/Renters Insurance:

This insurance covers cost associated with damage(s) to your home.

Key Word

A person gets **Homeowners insurance** if they have purchased their house or have a mortgage (borrowed to buy). **Fairly expensive.**

This covers:
House and other buildings (this covers cost to repair or replace your house)
Personal Property
Liability
Living Expenses

(Houses are such a large cost without insurance a disaster could cause financial ruin).

Renters Insurance

Costs	Benefits
• Another cost to pay for each month. • Deductibles mean you will still pay when damages occurs.	• Fairly inexpensive. • Covers the cost related to damage, theft or weather harming your things.

Homeowners Insurance

Costs	Benefits
• Large premium costs each month to stay insured. • Deductibles are often high when replacing things like the roof.	• Covers a lot of different costs. • The cost of fixing a house is very expensive and this helps with costs.

Our homes are a special place and the things in them matter to us. That is why insurance for **Personal Property** is so important! Items that are **stolen** or are **damaged** by weather they can get repaired or replaced if you have the right type of insurance!

Try to think of examples for each of these **different items covered by personal property coverage** and guess at their worth!

Clothing	Furniture	Electronics	Outdoor Stuff
Ex. Shoes $100			
Art & Collectibles	**Kitchen Items**	**Tools**	**Jewelry**

Renting

Owning a Home

What are the costs and benefits of renting a place to live?

Costs	Benefits

What are the costs and benefits of purchasing a house?

Costs	Benefits

Planning ahead can help prevent damage or reduce how serious a problem becomes. Share some ways you could **prevent the damage** that comes with these disasters or reduce the amount of damage that could happen?

Robbery	Fire	Storm	Accidents

Who provides for your family? What is an inheritance?

A person gets **life insurance** to protect the people who rely on them. If the person who pays the bills were to pass away, how would their family get by? They would need money to help them recover.

Life Insurance:
This insurance helps a person prepare for the financial costs related to their passing and provides support for their dependents in their absence.

Key Word

Life insurance helps families during a difficult time, giving them the **financial support** they need to process their loss and find their new normal.

Important:
This insurance is **not required** by the government, yet when dealing with risk it can be a helpful solution.

GC Sharp GC Sharp GC Sharp

So who gets the money? When a person is signing the contract they need to identify the **beneficiary**.

Beneficiary:
The person who receives the life insurance after the policyholder passes away.

"If I were to pass away unexpectedly, I want my children to have support to accomplish their dreams."

Here are the 2 major types: →

Term Life Insurance:
Life insurance is where you pay for coverage over a set time (term). It's often very affordable when you are younger, but the cost rises with age when renewing. Many people drop it at older ages because of the high cost.

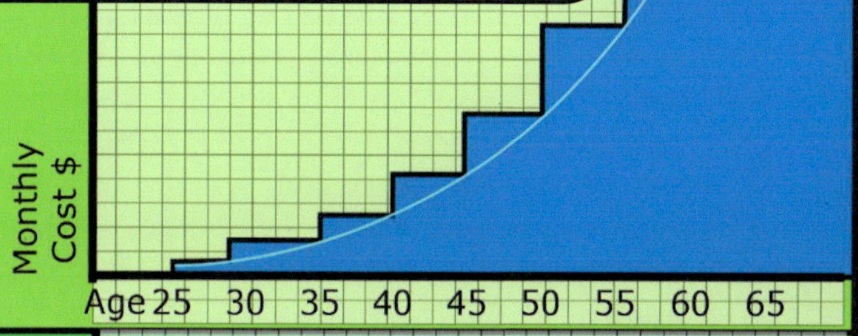

Permanent Insurance:
Life insurance is where you pay the same amount from start to finish, and the coverage continues as long as you pay. Sometimes, it builds cash value that you can use during your lifetime.

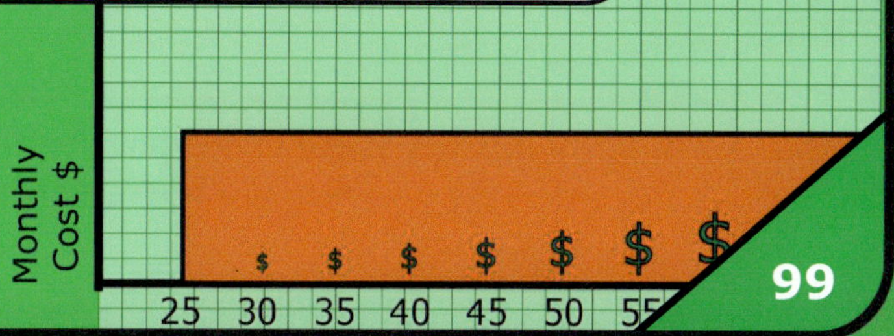

One of the risks of life is that at some point it ends. This is a reality of our lives. However, when it happens makes a big difference! This why **life insurance** is there to help those who rely on you! When you apply for life insurance you have to answer several questions and **fill out a contract**.

Here are some questions you may be asked when applying for insurance!

(Only answer what you feel comfortable with)

Age: (Generally insurance is more expensive the younger you are)	**Gender:** (Men have higher rates, because men on average live shorter lives)	**Do you smoke or vape?** ☐ Yes ☐ No (Smoking will increase premiums)
How would you describe your health? ☐ Excellent ☐ Good ☐ Fair	**How often do you exercise?** ☐ A lot ☐ Sometimes ☐ Not much	**How would you rate your stress level?** ☐ Low ☐ Medium ☐ High
Do you wear a seatbelt in the car? ☐ Always ☐ Sometimes ☐ Rarely	**Do you play sports?** ☐ Yes ☐ No	**If Yes, what sports?**

Here is what a contract may sound like. Fill it out like it's real!

Name of the Beneficiary (Who would receive the money if something happened to you.)

Beneficiary Name: **Relationship to You:**

I promise that the information above is true and the beneficiary I chose is correct.

I agree that my beneficiary is the person listed above.

Signature: **Date:**

Term means only for a period of time. If you are young and have a spouse or children, you might consider this because of its low cost and high coverage. Many people drop it later in life when their children can provide for themselves.

Check out how the connection between **premium, age & coverage.** (per month)

Age	Premium	Coverage	Cash Value
20	$17	$500,000	$0
30	$18	$500,000	$0
40	$28	$500,000	$0
50	$68	$500,000	$0
60	$195	$500,000	$0
70	$808	$500,000	$0

Why does term get more expensive over time?

Permanent means it lasts for your entire life. If you are young and want to build money you can use later or leave to your spouse or children, this type of insurance helps you do that over time.

*These examples are simplified to show how term and permanent insurance can work over time.

Check out how the connection between **premium, age, coverage & cash value.**

Age	Premium	Coverage	Cash Value
20	$250	$500,000	Very little
30	$250	$500,000	$20,000
40	$250	$500,000	$50,000
50	$250	$500,000	$100,000
60	$250	$500,000	$200,000
70	$250	$500,000	$350,000

What would you use the cash value to buy?

That is a lot to take in! How does a person keep all this organized?
That is why they have **agents** like myself and Doyle to help explain and organize much of this for you. When it comes to handling risk you will be happy to have a helper.
DT-7G
Evelyn, thank you so much for helping walk us through insurance. I feel like I can relax, knowing I have a way to handle the risk. We had best get to our spaceship and set course for Mars!
Take care and call if you need any help?

I don't know about you, but I feel more informed and better prepared for the unknown. However, Doyle seemed awfully familiar to me, like I had met him before...
Beep-Beep-Beeeep!
Exactly! I couldn't have said it better myself!
Hey don't forget the paperwork I gave you! Safe travels!
U.S.S. FLANNERY
1988

Doyle left with us some policies to fill out! Looks like the first one is how to handle stress and the second is for risk.

My Stress Policy: (How I will handle stress in my life)

Policy Holder:

Starting Date (Today):

Stress is a normal part of life.

It happens when I feel pressure, worry, or strong emotions.

This policy explains how I will handle stress in a healthy way.

My Stress Warning Signs

When I am stressed, I might:

- ☐ Feel frustrated or overwhelmed
- ☐ Get quiet or angry
- ☐ Have trouble focusing
- ☐ Feel tense or tired
- ☐ Want to avoid things

What I Will NOT Do

When I am stressed, I will try not to:

- ☐ Yell or lash out
- ☐ Make risky choices
- ☐ Give up
- ☐ Ignore the problem

My Stress Plan (TFB)

STOP. SCAN. PLAN

Thoughts	Feelings	Behaviors
When I notice stress, I will try to think:	**When I feel stressed, I will:** ☐ Take deep breaths ☐ Name how I feel ☐ Give myself time to calm down ☐ Other:	**When stress shows up, I will:** ☐ Walk away & cool down ☐ Talk to someone I trust ☐ Take a break ☐ Other:

My Stress Support Person

When I feel stressed, I can talk to:
Name:

How they can help me:

My Stress Promise

**"When I feel stressed,
I will try my best to handle it in a healthy way."**

Signature:

My Risk Policy: (How I will handle risk in my life)

Risk is anything that could cause harm or lead to a bad outcome if I don't think ahead.

This policy explains how I will recognize risk, think it through, and make safer choices.

My Risk Warning Signs

When I might be facing a risk, I might:

- ☐ Feel pressured by others
- ☐ Feel unsure or rushed
- ☐ Want to act without thinking
- ☐ Feel nervous
- ☐ Feel like something "doesn't feel right"

When I recognize Risk I will:

- ☐ Stop: Pause and slow down
- ☐ Think: Consider what could happen
- ☐ Share: Talk to someone I trust
- ☐ Act: Choose the safest option

Answer how you will be handling risk with STARR power:

Sharing	Transfering	Avoiding	Retaining	Reducing
I can share risk by asking for help or working with others, such as:	I can transfer risk by letting someone more responsible or experienced handle it, such as:	I can avoid risk by staying away from situations that could cause harm, such as:	I retain risk when I choose to accept it and be responsible, such as:	I reduce risk by making safer choices, such as:

My Risk Promise

"When I face risk, I will think before I act, use the STARR method, and make choices that help keep me safe."

Signature:

Step 4:

Investigate insurance and fill out policies for stress and risk.

Thank you so much for joining us on this journey!
DT-7G

Let's look back at your journey. Did you meet your goals?

Step 1:
Recognize how stress can cause us to react.

Step 2:
Understand how thoughts, feelings and behaviors are connected.

Step 3:
Identify the ways a person can handle risk personally and financially.

Step 4:
Investigate insurance and fill out policies for stress and risk.

Our Goal:
Learn strategies for handling **risk** and **stress** in our lives.

Did we meet our goal? Why or why not?

Flight is when you want to attack! True or False?

True

False

What is the answer?

If you are allergic to strawberries you use which way of handling risk?

Retain

Reduce

Avoid

Share

What is the answer?

Insurance is a key part of managing risk when it comes to money. Why do people need insurance?

Journal ...

In this lesson, you explored **how to handle stress and risk**. You did this by learning about your body's reaction to stress and how to protect yourself from financial risk.

How do you think growing in these areas could make your life better?

Journal to see your TFB!

Purchase a journal where you can record your private thoughts and feelings.

- Plan for a time you can regularly write about your life.
- Share with an adult if you want help problem solving.

Explore the Store!

Next time you're at The Store:

- **Stop! Scan! Plan!**

Walk through the important questions before you make a purchase.

What are the facts?
What are you thinking? Feeling?
What can you control?
What are your options?

Mind & Money!

Be a Risk Recognizer!

- This week observe the level of risk around you. If you are driving by a construction site, where are the danger zones?
- Then try to identify how people are handling the risk!

The Game of Risk!

This is a classic game of strategy! In it your goal is to conquer the ground other players hold. For younger children consider playing the junior version of it.

- Every choice you make has its costs and benefits!

The Galactic Growth journey will continue!
Until we meet again, take care and spread kindness everywhere!

Flight is when you want to attack! True or False?

False

Fight is when you want to attack. Flight is when your body tells you to run and hide. When we can read how we are feeling it can help us understand what to do next!

If you are allergic to strawberries you use which way of handling risk?

Avoid

When you are allergic it means you have a reaction to something. Some people this can be dangerous, so it is best to avoid it!

Insurance is a key part of managing risk when it comes to money. Why do people need insurance?

These are many reason why people need insurance. The biggest one is that major cost related to health, vehicles and property are so big most people couldn’t handle them alone. Insurance allows you to pay a smaller amount and reduce your financial risk.

What's next?

You can continue the journey by joining us for the rest of the series. You rock for making your knowledge about **mind** & **money** a priority!

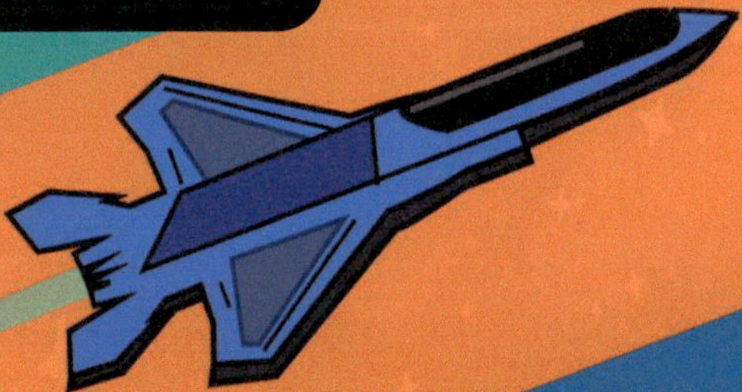

Glossary

Here you can find all of the major terms discussed in this book!

Avoid Risk	**60**	When you find ways to not experience the risk.
Behaviors	**36**	The actions that a person does. These actions can be intentional or reactive.
Beneficiary	**99**	The person who receives the life insurance after the policyholder passes away.
Car Insurance	**90**	This is insurance that covers cost related to car accidents and other damage to your car.
Cause and Effect	**18**	When one thing happens (the cause), it leads to something else happening (the effect).
Claim	**82**	A request you make to your insurance company to help pay for costs after something covered by your policy happen, like an accident or damage.
Collision Insurance	**91**	This covers the cost of repair for your vehicle in the case that you hit another car or object that causes damage.
Comprehensive Insurance	**91**	This covers the cost for most things that could harm your vehicle other than a collision.
Cost and Benefits	**55**	A system where you compare the positive and negative consequences of a choice.
Coverage	**80**	The specific events, situations, or types of damage that your insurance policy will cover.
Deductible	**78**	What you agree to pay before insurance will cover the cost. This helps reduce your monthly costs, yet adds to your out of pocket financial risk!
Fawn	**22**	When you try to please others to avoid conflict or danger.
Feelings	**32**	The ability to sense your emotions.
Fight	**20**	Your body thinks it's in danger and reacts by getting ready to attack to protect itself.
Flight	**20**	Your body senses danger and tries to escape or avoid the threat.
Freeze	**22**	When your body shuts down or feels stuck.
Habit	**38**	A habit is something you do regularly, often without thinking.
HALT	**34**	Hungry, Angry, Lonely and Tired. Times you should careful with your actions.

Health Insurance	**86**	Insurance that covers the costs related to medical needs and emergencies.
Home/Renters Insurance:	**94**	This is insurance covers cost associated with damage(s) to your home.
Insurance	**71**	An agreement between a person and a company to share the risk of financial loss.
Liability Insurance	**91**	This covers the debt a person would owe for damage to a person's property and injuries.
Life Insurance:	**98**	Insurance that helps a person prepare for the financial costs related to their passing.
Living Expenses	**94**	Insurance for costs if you can't live where you are renting.
Negativity Bias	**30**	The mind naturally focuses more attention on negative experiences or information.
Permanent Insurance:	**99**	Life insurance where you pay the same amount from start to finish, and coverage continues as long as you pay.
Personal Property	**94**	Insurance for repairing or replacing your belongings.
Policy	**76**	Coverage that outlines each party's responsibility and the terms and conditions.
Premium	**76**	This is the amount that you pay the insurance company per month to be covered.
Reduce Risk	**64**	When you find and use ways to make the risk less.
Retain Risk	**62**	When you recognize the risk and choose to not change it.
Risk	**9**	The chance of gain or loss associated with a situation or choice.
Self Talk	**29**	The thoughts and words you tell yourself every day.
Self-Discipline	**51**	The ability to control one's actions and stay focused on one's goals.
Self-Management	**15**	The ability to manage your own emotions, thoughts, and behaviors to achieve goals.
Sharing Risk	**56**	When you take on risk with another person or group.
STARR	**54**	A person can share, transfer, avoid, retain or reduce risk.
Stop. Scan. Plan	**42**	A pattern a person can use to make wise decisions.
Stress	**16**	The body's response to physical, mental, or emotional pressure.
Term Life Insurance:	**99**	Life insurance where you pay for coverage over a set time (term).
The TFB in Me	**26**	The process of recognizing the cycle of thoughts, feelings and behaviors.
Thoughts	**28**	Ideas that are being processed in your mind.
Transfer Risk	**58**	When you are able to give someone else your risk.

Car Cutout

- Color and design
- Cut around the outside
- Fold
- Tape or staple

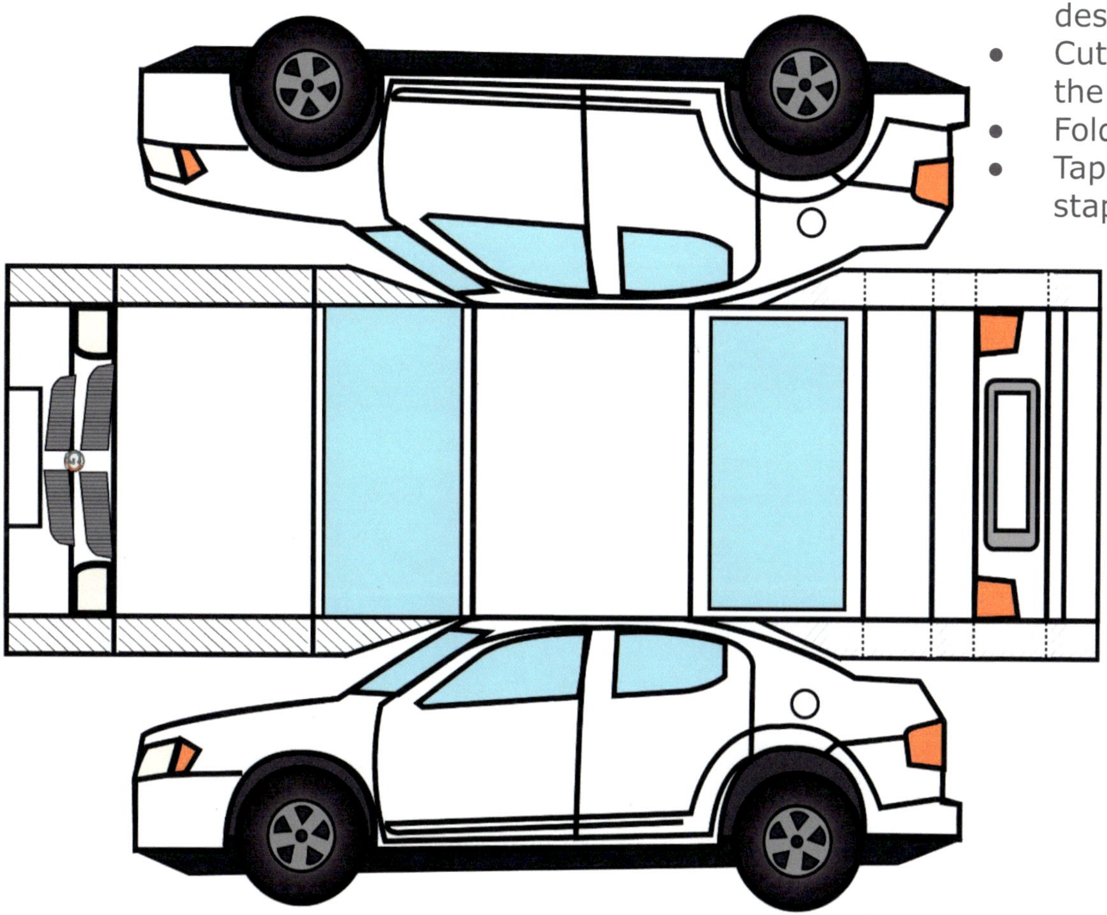

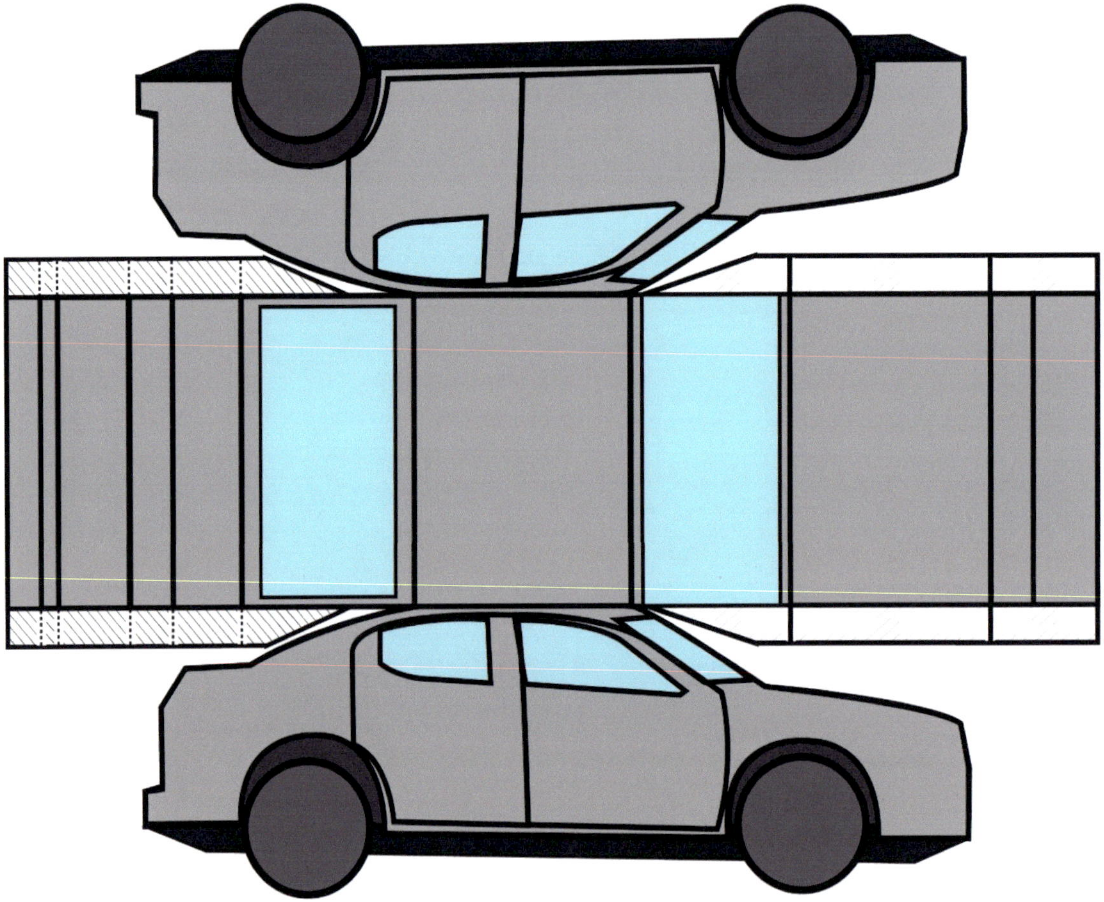

Made in the USA
Las Vegas, NV
03 November 2026

57424186R00076